Inhabiting Physical Culture

We are looking at a series of black-and-white photographs. Three young women sit cross-legged, side by side on the floor of a large, open room, their backs turned to a bank of enormous windows that flood the space with light. The lush foliage of a well-kept winter garden on the far side of the room stands in stark contrast to the bare branches of the trees dotting the hillside beyond the glass, a clear indication that it is winter. All the more curious, then, that the room's inhabitants are only half-dressed, each with only a thin exercise mat to insulate her from the chill of the floor. Their postures are rigid as they hoist medicine balls overhead, eyes fixed on the swirling texture of the stone-clad wall opposite them.

A fourth young woman stands behind them, steadying herself with one hand against the curved flange of a cruciform column. Its polished chrome surface is, we imagine, cold to the touch. She settles the medicine ball against her hip, shifting her weight away from the column to stretch the muscles of her lower back. Around the edge of the partition, in the shadows of the next room, we glimpse another silhouette—their instructor en route to supervise their afternoon regimen.

This scene unfolded in February 1956, indelibly captured by the young photographer Miloš Budík on the ground floor of 45 Černopolní Street in Brno, in what was then Czechoslovakia—Mies van der Rohe's Villa Tugendhat (Fig. 1–7). The world was a far different place than it had been when local industrialists Grete and Fritz Tugendhat, having earlier been introduced to Mies's work by friend and noted German art historian Eduard Fuchs, first approached the architect in 1928 to commission the design of their new family home. The couple and their three young children moved into the completed house, a striking realization of Mies's increasingly sophisticated ideas about modern domestic design, merely two years later. But the happiness the Tugendhat family would find there proved to be tragically short-lived. In July 1938, the growing threat of invasion by German forces left the family no choice but to flee the country, first to Switzerland, and later to England. They would never again reside in the house that has left their family name inscribed in the canon of modern architecture.

The building was harshly treated during the war, first by German troops, then Soviet. Different areas of the house are said to have been repurposed to serve a variety of functions during the conflict: an officers' headquarters, a barracks, and even, it is said, a stables in the main living space. Materials were pilfered or damaged as control of Brno shifted, such that by the end of the war many of the house's signature features had either vanished or been marred beyond recognition. The half-cylindrical partition encircling the dining area, clad in a richly colored ebony wood veneer, disappeared not long after the family's departure. In the main living space, many of the monolithic glass panes of the glass facade were presumably broken, and the immaculate white linoleum floor tiles were damaged beyond repair. By all accounts the house was in a state of semi-ruin when Karla Hladká, a local dance instructor who also taught in the nearby conservatory, established a private dance school there in 1945.

It is reasonable to assume that it was Hladká's occupation of the house that provoked the earliest repairs, although the outcome bore little resemblance to the luxurious material vocabulary Mies had so painstakingly specified during its initial construction. Nowhere was this more clearly articulated than in the main living space. The cost of replacing the original monolithic glass windows must have been prohibitively expensive, so their replacements consisted of gridded steel frames supporting smaller glass panes.[1] The remnants of the white linoleum floor were removed entirely, and the subfloor was covered by a xylolite screed in vivid red.[2] The awkward void left by the removal of the curved ebony wall was filled with a series of linear partitions stepping back towards the door to the patio, using the previously free-standing cruciform columns to produce strange corner details (a gesture one hopes may have amused Mies, if only for its irony).

For the next five years, the students of Karla Hladká's Institute of Physical Culture, primarily young children, would utilize the house's spacious rooms and generous terraces as stages for their training. Though the school's existence was short-lived, this period seems to have established a powerful precedent for the perceived utility of the house in the public imagination, as evidenced by its subsequent uses. After the school's closure in June of 1950, the house was briefly administered by the State Institute of Curative Gymnastics, after which ownership passed to the municipality of Brno. Only then was the Villa Tugendhat transformed into a spinal rehabilitation clinic for the local children's hospital, a program that remained unchanged for the better part of thirty years. Gymnastic equipment was mounted against walls where the family's art collection must have once hung. Mr. and Mrs. Tugendhat's rooms were transformed into offices, examination rooms, and surgeries. The children's bedrooms were filled with cots, where young patients received regular educational instruction while resting in corrective postures. The longevity of this arrangement suggests that the house must have worked marvelously in fulfilling its new program. Indeed, one imagines that, by this time, the relatively brief period in which the family had made their home there must have seemed a distant memory.

Villa Tugendhat was one of the formative achievements of Mies's career (and, one might argue, in the broader scheme of modern architecture) before the outbreak of the Second World War. With its free-flowing floor plan, ingenious operable windows, trademark cruciform columns, and a material palette that was equal parts sumptuous and severe, it redefined the domestic vocabulary of what had, to that point, been an ostensibly functionalist modern architecture. How strange, then, that it should be resuscitated not as a house at all, but as a dance studio, then a space of physical therapy. On the other hand, perhaps the transformation should be viewed as somewhat obvious. The very qualities that have inscribed the project in both the modern canon and contemporary architectural imagination, the particular tension generated by its combination of materials and forms, may very well have been the source of this curious adaptation—perceived as the trappings of a space intended for what had been called, as Hladká's school so evocatively pronounced, *physical culture*. And so, Villa Tugendhat, for a time anyway, became exactly that: a gymnasium.

How could this conflation have emerged in the first place? Did modern architects consciously take the gymnasium of the previous century as a point of departure in imagining a new domestic environment? Or maybe this striking coincidence of tropes stemmed from a reciprocal exchange between the gymnasium and the house during the interwar period. After all, the modern architecture of the 1920s and '30s was above all characterized by a sweeping reconsideration of the rituals of daily life, and therefore often involved radical typological experimentation. The question of the *modern house*, so central to the architectural discourse of the era, was fundamentally intertwined with a preoccupation with the *modern body*. So it should come as no surprise that physical culture—by then a fully formed phenomenon with sweeping cultural implications—became increasingly drawn towards the center of a new domestic paradigm. But to fully appreciate the significance of physical culture in these years, how it initially came into dialogue with modern architecture, and why it matters, we must first understand how it began to take shape during the 18th and 19th centuries, both practically and ideologically.

—

> "Do you, then, want to cultivate your pupil's intelligence? Cultivate the strengths it ought to govern. Exercise his body continually; make him robust and healthy in order to make him wise and reasonable. Let him work, be active, run, yell, always be in motion. Let him be a man in his vigor, and soon he will be one in his reason."[3]

Etymologically speaking, long before the idea of *physical culture*, even before the advent of *sport*, there was *gymnastics*.[4] While regimens of physical exercise have obviously existed throughout human history, they have largely been synonymous with military pursuits.[5] This began to change somewhat during the Industrial Revolution, a period that witnessed an unprecedented migration of populations from the countryside to the city. The formation of a new urban populace, and the arrival of a new kind of citizen—the factory worker—planted the seeds that would blossom into mass culture during the 19th century. This remarkable reorganization of the social and economic order demanded the dramatic reimagining of nearly every aspect of daily life. The period was concerned with the development of new methods of education and new forms of recreation, tasks which would ultimately become intertwined both with one another and with a growing anxiety about society's sudden disconnect from nature. Inspired by the humanist ideals of the Enlightenment, a shift towards a more codified and popular gymnastics began to take shape, driven by a growing association between physical exercise, and both intellectual and moral development. In this last regard, the influence of Rousseau, particularly his ideas about *natural education*, cannot be overstated.

> "To exercise an art, one must begin by procuring for oneself the instruments for it; and, to be able to employ these instruments usefully, one has to make them solid enough to resist wear. To learn to think, therefore, it is necessary to exercise our limbs, our senses, our organs, which are the instruments of our intelligence. And, to get the greatest possible advantage from these instruments, the body which provides them must be robust and healthy. Thus, far from man's true reason being formed independently of the body, it is the body's good constitution which makes the mind's operations easy and sure."[6]

Rousseau's emphasis on the importance of bodily exercise to the sharpening of the intellect served as the unmistakable inspiration for a sequence of educational reformers who championed the integration of gymnastics into curricula in the second half of the 18th century. In 1774, Johann Bernard Basedow founded a progressive school in Dessau. This endeavor, which he dubbed the Philanthropinum, quickly found support among both an "enlightened" local aristocracy and key members of the German intelligentsia (Goethe was an early and vocal advocate, and Kant would later acknowledge the school's influence on his own ideas about education).[7] Drawing upon Rousseau, Basedow was convinced that the development of the body was fundamental to the cultivation of the mind. He became among the first to teach gymnastics and calisthenics as part of an educational curriculum, and was known for leading his students on long hikes through the countryside.[8] Although Basedow's tenure as director of the Philanthropinum, and indeed the life of the school itself, were relatively brief, the progression of this experiment served as a crucial touchstone for new models of education in the years to follow.[9]

Among those following Basedow's work was another German innovator, Johann Christoph Friedrich GutsMuths, who published his seminal textbook *Gymnastik für die Jugend* (Gymnastics for the Youth) in 1792 (Fig. 8). Formulated around the Greek pentathlon, as well as several exercises of his own design, it was the first book to systematize gymnastic exercise for a mass audience. For GutsMuths, physical exercise was both scientific—he insisted that the most crucial criteria of his teaching method was *measurability*—and poetic.[10] In his own words, it was a "culture for the body"—a physical culture, if you will, though this name wouldn't catch on until the 20th century—which represented a crucial contribution to the holistic development of the individual, providing discipline and self-control.[11] The text established GutsMuths as the preeminent authority on gymnastics during his lifetime.

The book also became an indispensable point of reference for a younger generation of innovators. In 1799, Franz Nachtegall established a private gymnasium in Copenhagen, the first facility of its kind in Europe not affiliated with a school.[12] Nachtegall adapted both GutsMuths' curriculum of running, jumping, and balancing, and his preferred system of equipment, comprising a variety of wooden horses, climbing masts, hanging ropes, and ladders.[13] His studious reproduction of GutsMuths' methodology proved to be incredibly successful, and by 1805 his gymnasium boasted more than a hundred students, among them a young Per Henrik Ling.

A native of Sweden, Ling had traveled extensively throughout Europe, studying theology and linguistics before discovering GutsMuths' writings. His growing interest in gymnastics led him to Denmark to train with Nachtegall, and then to return to Sweden in 1808 to teach gymnastics and fencing at the University of Lund. Five years later, he founded the Gymnastiska Centralinstitutet (Royal Central Gymnastics Institute) in Stockholm, and served as its principal for the remainder of his life. Ling innovated a distinctly Swedish form of gymnastics, expanding upon both GutsMuths' writings and Nachtegall's teachings, but discarding many of the more cumbersome devices championed by his predecessors. Recognizing that one body invariably differed from the next, Ling advocated for a system defined above all by freedom of movement and adaptability. To that end, he invented a number of enduring gymnastic devices that were simpler in both form and application, including the wall bars, the beams, and the box horse.[14] In contrast to his contemporaries, Ling also placed greater emphasis on choreographed group exercises led by an instructor (Fig. 9–11), an aspect of his teachings that simultaneously reinforced the communal aspect of gymnastics, and underscored its lingering connections to military discipline.[15]

Another of Ling's enduring contributions was his adamant belief that his methods offered concrete medical benefits to practitioners, though his advocacy for these supposed benefits was initially met with skepticism from the scientific community. Perhaps the single greatest measure of his importance, both to Swedish culture and to the broader development of modern physical culture, was that he was eventually admitted to the Swedish General Medical Association in 1831—in effect, an acknowledgement of the validity of his claims.[16] That Ling's methods were ultimately rational in both their formulation and their aims suggests something of an ideological break with the moralistic impulses of his German predecessors. Indeed, thanks in no small part to Ling's contributions, gymnastics would become increasingly understood as a fundamentally hygienic pursuit in this period.

Along with Ling, the most significant innovator in the development of 19th-century gymnastics is indisputably Friedrich Jahn.[17] Whereas Basedow and GutsMuths were explicitly concerned with bending gymnastics to the cultivation of the individual, Jahn recognized it as an instrument of radical political potential. As a veteran of the Napoleonic Wars arriving in Berlin in 1810, Jahn was deeply humiliated by the Prussian defeat and subsequent French occupation. He promoted gymnastics as a "lifeline of the German people," capable of restoring not only the physical strength but also the moral character of his as-yet fragmented country.[18] In keeping with this nativist formulation, Jahn refused to employ foreign words for his methods—he rejected "gymnastics," opting instead for the more Teutonic *turnen*.[19]

In 1811, Jahn opened his so-called Turnplatz in Berlin (Fig. 12). An open-air precursor to the modern gymnasium, the Turnplatz was a painstakingly planned sequence of novel devices for gymnastics, many of Jahn's own invention. It was, significantly, also a hotbed of political activity. Over the years, Jahn developed something of a cult of personality, and his disciples—or *turners*—consisted largely of young men dedicated to the expulsion of the French and, after the occupation had ended, to the establishment of a new revolutionary government. The image of the Turnplatz—of young turners sharpening their bodies in ways never before seen, all while talking openly of revolution—clearly struck Jahn's conservative political adversaries as a threat, a fact made quite clear by the intensity of their reprisal.[21] Following the assassination of the conservative writer August von Kotzebue by student activist Karl Ludwig Sand in 1819, the German Confederation began to crack down on centers of revolutionary thought. Under the Carlsbad Decrees, the Turnplatz was closed, and Jahn—by that time a highly visible advocate for the cause of German unification—was arrested and imprisoned at Spandau until 1824, effectively ending his active influence on what was by then beginning to resemble modern physical culture.[22]

Jahn's impact on political thought, including the degree to which gymnastics became increasingly identified with the cause of German unification, represents a crucial precursor to the later, more significant shift of the so-called "cult of the body" towards the center of German public life. For Jahn, the cultivation of the body was, above all, the ostensible precondition for a nation capable of withstanding future aggression and preventing future occupation. His teachings were built around a revolutionary brand of populism, one that differed dramatically from any contemporary understanding of the word, insofar as it advocated for liberal democracy as a means to break with the conservative, rigidly class-based hierarchies that had defined European societies up to that point. His philosophy was fundamentally built around a notion of patriotism that prioritized both individual freedom and egalitarianism.

But Jahn's ideas ultimately drew much of their power by gesturing towards a troubling, as yet unnamed seed of nationalist ideology. By the time of Germany's unification in 1871, the

Aryan myth had influenced an entire generation of politically motivated thinkers, who perverted theories outlined in Darwin's *On the Origin of Species* (1859) and Max Müller's *Lectures on the Science of Language* (1861) to insist on the supposed primacy of Germanic culture and the German body—in Jahn's case, the militarized body of the German man. While highly controversial in academic circles, Aryanism nonetheless enjoyed growing popularity with the German public, and gradually became conflated with a sense of patriotism. In time, this development would become a disturbing ideological undercurrent not only for some proponents of physical culture, but also for other movements that professed to be rooted in scientific or rational thought, including eugenics.[23]

Finally, standing somewhat apart from this otherwise direct lineage of innovators of physical culture, was the French theater instructor François Delsarte. Not only were his contributions conceived for the stage rather than the gymnasium, his association with the broader movement of physical culture was in many ways the outcome of misinterpretation. Born in northern France, Delsarte began his training as a vocal student in the Paris Conservatory, only to have his singing career brought to an abrupt end when illness badly damaged his vocal cords. Deprived of a career on the stage, he turned to teaching. While he initially focused on training other singers, Delsarte became increasingly preoccupied with what he considered a lack of emotional truth in the acting method taught in the Conservatory. He soon turned his energies to developing a new method of instruction for actors—one built around the theory that emotional and mental states were intrinsically linked to physical posture, expression, and gesture. That is, the performer could powerfully and precisely communicate a range of emotions to an audience through the controlled movement of the body.[24]

To formulate his system of *applied aesthetics*, Delsarte studied anatomy, philosophy, and political theory.[25] Much like Ling, he asserted that his approach was fundamentally scientific—a search for an objective, rational basis for theater.[26] Against the tide of specialization sweeping through academia, Delsarte insisted on a more synthetic understanding of performance. He spoke of *art* rather than *the arts*, of *science* rather than *the sciences*.[27] He rejected narrow ideas of technique in favor of a performance that drew upon many forms of learning. The approach proved to be incredibly successful. During his lifetime, he attracted students from throughout Europe, including numerous well-known actors of the period, as well as artists, clergy, and writers.[28]

Despite his popularity in France, the longevity of Delsarte's influence was thrown into doubt when he died in 1871 without having published a book of his collected teachings. While Delsarte's protégé and designated intellectual heir, the American actor and playwright Steele MacKaye, would go on to disseminate his ideas in the United States to some fanfare, it was ultimately one of MacKaye's American pupils, the actress Genevieve Stebbins, who would publish the first book of Delsarte's teachings. *The Delsarte System of Expression*, published in 1885, combined the underlying theory of Delsarte's teachings with clear instructions and illustrations. The book was an immediate sensation in the United States, setting into motion one of the earliest modern fitness movements, and allowing Stebbins to build a career as the eminent authority, along with MacKaye, on the methods of the late, suddenly fashionable Delsarte. But the popularity and commercial viability of Stebbins's book led to a multitude of imitators and self-styled experts, countless "Delsarte clubs," badly written instruction manuals, and even specialty clothing for what was increasingly promoted as a form of "aesthetic gymnastics." Ironically, this conflation of Delsarte's deeply theorized method of performance with an exercise of hollow posing led to its gradual dilution and ultimate disavowal by a new generation of thespians. While his influence began to fade by the turn of the century, Delsarte's methods had nonetheless already made an impression on the earliest innovators of modern dance, including Ted Shawn, Isadora Duncan, and Rudolf von Laban.[29] More importantly, the widespread popularity of his teachings, however misinterpreted, had established a strong link between theater, dance, and gymnastic exercise in the public imagination, an association that would ultimately prove integral to the formulation of modern physical culture.

By the turn of the 20th century, the movements of the preceding centuries had given way to something far richer and more complex than mere gymnastics. At this crucial inflection point, it was no longer simply about what was *natural*, per Rousseau, but rather a question of what was *modern*. Emerging in concert with a broader modern movement, the aptly named physical culture was both scientific and poetic, intimate yet collective, and physical, intellectual, and spiritual all at once. Crucially, it was now facilitated by a rich universe of distinctive objects and equipment, increasingly mechanical, designed to enhance both the experience and results of physical exercise. Significantly, unlike the gymnastics movements that had preceded it, the physical culture of the early 20th century had begun to operate in direct dialogue with art—moving ever closer to a form of creative expression, even as it was increasingly embraced by the scientific community as crucial to health and hygiene. In all of this complexity, in its numerous forms, physical culture had begun to take its place as one of the indispensable rituals of modern life.

"Palucca's dances, von Laban's motion choirs, and Mensendieck's functional gymnastics have surpassed the aesthetic eroticism of the painted nude. The stadium has carried the day against the art museum, just as bodily reality has taken the place of beautiful illusion. Sport unifies the individual with the masses. Sport is becoming the advanced school of collective feeling."[30]

The physical culture of the Weimar Republic was, not unlike modern architecture itself, framed in altogether more utopian terms than what had come before. It was, above all, about liberation—the power of unencumbered social, sexual, and creative expression, coupled with emerging industrial technology, to establish new codes of behavior, new political structures, and a more rational and humane society. This idealistic, even zealous belief in the power of *the new* to carry society past the devastation of the First World War is made abundantly clear in "The New World," an essay published by the Swiss-born architect Hannes Meyer in 1926, only a year after he was appointed head of the newly established architecture department at the Bauhaus. The essay was, in effect, a manifesto for his nascent radical-functionalist, anti-aesthetic philosophy of design, later dubbed *Die neue Baulehre*, or "the new way to build." One of the text's more ecstatic observations addressed the emergence of a new and distinctly modern fascination with sport. For Meyer, this phenomenon had already superseded art as the driving force of mass culture, and he asserted that this triumph—of physicality over representation, of collectivism over elitism, of empiricism over formalism—was evident in the widespread popularity of German physician Bess Mensendieck's system of therapeutic gymnastics (Fig. 13), Hungarian dance instructor

Von Laban's applied theories of movement ("motion choirs"), and Bauhaus associate Gret Palucca's progressive choreography (Fig. 14).[31, 32] Meyer was, above all, concerned with the collectivizing potential of sport.[33] He described this phenomenon, rather unforgettably, as *(die) hohen Schule des Kollektivgefühls* (roughly, "the advanced school of collective feeling").[34]

Shortly after succeeding Walter Gropius as director of the Bauhaus in 1928, Meyer and his partner Hans Wittwer began work on the design of the ADGB Trade Union School in Bernau.[35] A fixation on sport is evident in the basic scheme of the project, which prominently features a gymnasium outfitted with modern fitness equipment and a running track circling a pond on the grounds. It is clear from his writings that Meyer believed the integration of "body culture" into everyday life to be an inevitable condition of modernity (he included "personal hygiene" as one of the core programs of the modern home in his essay "Bauen," or "Building," published that same year).[36] Taken as a whole, the ADGB School keeps with Meyer's conviction about the transformative power of industry, technology, novelty, and mass culture articulated in "The New World." The forms and arrangement of buildings, as well as the deft synthesis of concrete, steel, and masonry construction, represent one of the most coherent and memorable expressions of his functionalist philosophy. And yet the gymnasium is somehow out of sync with this transformative vision, possibly because it so sharply recalls Jahn's Turnplatz of a century earlier. Photographs of the ADGB gymnasium (Fig. 15) reveal nominally updated equipment first devised in the 19th century—rings, beams, bars, pommel horses, and other inventions by Ling and Jahn. Despite his belief in sport as a collectivizing force, Meyer, along with most designers of his day, seemed uninterested in reconsidering its material trappings or questioning the validity of its claims to universality—in *redesigning* physical culture, in other words, to include other bodies and render possible other embodiments of this modern spirit. Revolutionary rhetoric aside, the objects of 1920s physical culture were, in fact, heirlooms of the previous century, designed with a single body in mind: an able, militarized, invariably male body. This often meant awkwardness or discomfort for female practitioners, and outright exclusion (both physically and conceptually) for those with disabilities. And it must be observed that the basic forms of these objects have remained more or less untouched in the century since.

In spite of the problematic qualities made evident by a contemporary reading of early 20th century physical culture, the discourse then underlying this phenomenon was primarily concerned with its potential as a a catalyst for collectivity, or marked by a nearly utopian optimism about the liberating potential of the cultivation of the body. It was these progressive associations that allowed the modern notion of the body to reverberate far beyond the stadium, the gymnasium, and other more explicit spaces of physical culture. For instance, the biometric diagrams and building standards of Ernst Neufert's *Bauentwurfslehre*, first published in 1936, were likely influenced by these ideas. Significantly, this discourse also extended to new ideas about the domestic interior flourishing throughout the world, as some of modern architecture's most prominent figures attempted to rethink how physical culture might help to reconfigure the rhythms of the everyday, not merely as a collective activity, but also as a more private and individual pursuit. The question of *what makes a body modern*, and the often experimental spaces that took shape in an attempt to respond to it, led to a crucial development. That is, physical culture, and with it the material and spatial qualities of the gymnasium, began to infiltrate the modern home.

Marcel Breuer's contributions to this development are especially lucid. His earliest attempt to integrate physical culture with domestic space came in 1926, when he was commissioned to renovate the Berlin apartment of the famed avant-garde theater director Erwin Piscator and actress Hildegard Piscator (née Jurczyk) (Fig. 20–21). Though Breuer was extraordinarily young—he had completed his studies at the Bauhaus only two years before and was subsequently hired by Gropius as a young master in the school's carpentry workshop in 1925—he had already developed the earliest-known chromium steel furniture, including his now ubiquitous B3 chair. Breuer was therefore known primarily as a designer of objects, not of spaces, at the time of the commission. In fact, there's reason to believe that the apartment was his first architectural project without the involvement of Gropius, and his relative inexperience is legible in the surviving photographs of the apartment.[37, 38] His ability to compose a truly modern space was limited by the constraints of the existing apartment—he painted the walls pure white, stripped them of any ornament save a dark lacquered baseboard, and deployed his own cantilevered steel furniture throughout the project. The resulting space was, for modernists of the era, rather typical. What ultimately sets it apart from comparably scaled domestic projects of the period, and lends it what we believe to be a certain historical significance, is the provision of a miniature gymnasium in the bedroom. A set of gymnastic equipment—wall bars, a speed punching bag, medicine balls, and juggling pins—lined one side of the room. The opposite wall was dominated by a peculiar bed, which appears to have been designed to hide inside of a large, cabinet-like armature. The fact that the bed could disappear when the inhabitants wished it suggests that the more traditionally domestic program of the bedroom was subservient to a more innovative program: the home gym.[39]

The transformation of the bedroom into a space of physical culture (and vice versa) provides a useful framework for understanding Breuer's subsequent thinking. In 1930, he was commissioned to design the Berlin apartment of the gymnast Hilde Levi (Fig. 22). This project was quite different from the Piscator commission, as Levi intended for the apartment to double as a gymnastics studio not merely for personal use, but for instructing her students. Fortunately for Levi, Breuer's architectural instincts had, by this time, developed significantly. He divided the apartment into two halves, reducing the traditionally domestic programs to a carefully composed, utilitarian minimum—a modest working area equipped with bookshelves and a desk (chromium steel works of his own design, of course), a kitchenette, and a daybed for sleeping recessed between a walk-in closet and a bathroom. By condensing the living quarters so radically, Breuer was able to open the other half of the apartment into a large, sunken studio of roughly 36 square meters. In contrast to the wood-paneled walls of the domestic area, the walls of the studio were painted white, with dark, semi-reflective panels protecting their lower portion from the inevitable wear-and-tear they would sustain during Levi's gymnastics lessons. Breuer used the floors as another visual clue indicating the separation of programs—dark black for the domestic area, and stark white in the case of the gymnastics studio. And while surviving photographs depict the studio as open to the living space, plans indicate that these areas could be partitioned from one another by means of a collapsible sliding screen—providing privacy for Levi, eliminating visual distractions for students during lessons, and creating a remarkable degree of flexibility. It is not difficult to view this strategy as an expansion of his approach to the Piscator bedroom, with the gymnasium given priority and the domestic aspect of the project effortlessly hidden at the whim of the inhabitant. But the reorganization of domestic space in Levi's apartment also suggests a more dramatic shift in his philosophy: physical culture is no longer signified by a mere collection of objects, but is rather continuous with and a crucial aspect of the home.

Breuer's preoccupation with merging the gymnasium and the house would culminate at the Berlin Bauausstellung (Building Exposition) of 1931, where he unveiled a full-scale interior installation for his ambitious "House for a Sportsman" project (Fig. 23–25). Unlike in earlier works, here the separation of domestic space from the gymnasium is far more difficult to detect. Or perhaps it would be more accurate to say that the integration was far more complete, generating an altogether new type of environment. With the exception of a small bedroom and kitchen that are relegated to the edge of the house—indicated in his drawings, but not built as part of the installation—domestic programs, including a bathroom, dining area, and bedroom, along with a room for medical examination and therapeutic massage, are contained in a series of smaller, compartment-like rooms, arranged rhythmically to one side of a large central space. Equal in their modest scale, these spaces were almost clinical in character, separated from one another by thin partitions, and were interconnected by a corridor running along the rear of the rooms. As with Levi's gymnastics studio, these rooms could be hidden from the central space, this time by a series of folding textile screens. This sequence of more traditionally domestic or else specialized programs could be understood as a sort of "back of house," supporting the hybridized living room-gymnasium itself, which serves as the public-facing "stage."

The gymnasium itself is largely unadorned. While reminiscent of Levi's studio in its openness, it differs in that it is punctuated near its center by a heavy punching bag suspended from the ceiling. Nearly all available wall space is adorned with a variety of gymnastic equipment (speed bag, wall bars, wall-mounted chest pulley weights) in a manner similar to the bedroom of the Piscator apartment; a rowing machine sits in a far corner; a folding curtain demarcates a carpeted lounging area full of Breuer-designed furniture, allowing it to be separated, or not, from the gymnasium. Given the presumed lifestyle of the inhabitant, it is easy to imagine the folding screens going rarely used, the activities of a life centered around physical culture unfolding effortlessly and without interruption.

Breuer's preoccupation with physical culture was contemporaneous with his time at the Bauhaus, and he was not alone in this obsession. Enthusiasm for both competitive sports and a system of expressive bodily movement taught by Karla Grosch (a former student of Palucca who joined the Bauhaus staff in 1928) was central to the school's culture, embraced by students and faculty alike, such that it often carried over in their work. Gropius and Herbert Bayer, for example, joined Breuer in designing the German section of the Salon des Artistes Décorateurs in Paris in 1930, now commonly referred to as the Werkbund exhibition. Not unexpectedly, a set of wall bars and gymnastic rings linger just feet from a semi-circular bar made of chromed steel and lacquered wood, complete with Breuer-designed Thonet stools (Fig. 26–27).

Like Breuer, Gropius would go on to participate in the Bauausstellung exhibition the following year, displaying a speculative housing scheme in which the apartments themselves were conceived as small, minimal units, with a broad range of amenities collected at ground level. Built as a full-scale mock-up, these "communal rooms" contained, among other things, both a gymnasium and a swimming pool (Fig. 28). Photographs of the exhibition show marble-tiled floors and columns wrapped in mirrored panels—material choices that fit naturally into the language of the gymnasium, but that would also become among the most common tropes of modernism more broadly, even in the home.

A fascination with physical culture's relationship to housing extended beyond the walls of the Bauhaus, and in fact there's reason to believe that it had become an active point of discussion amongst the Deutscher Werkbund. Richard Döcker's contribution to the Mies-curated Weisenhoff Estate in Stuttgart of 1927 was notable for its inclusion of a simple gymnasium on the terrace, consisting of no more than a set of wall bars (Fig. 29). A polemicist and a member of *Der Ring*—along with Mies, Gropius, Hans Scharoun, and Hugo Häring, among many others—Döcker would go on to publish *Terrassen Typ* in 1929. The book featured striking photos of the terrace gymnasium in use by a young resident. That same year, perhaps inspired by Döcker's example, Theo Effenberger would include a slightly expanded terrace gymnasium in his contribution to the 1929 WuWA Estate in Breslau (modern Wrocław). Photos taken shortly after its completion depict a group of young women enjoying a sunny afternoon on their second-floor terrace, which boasts a set of wall bars and a speed punching bag suspended between the terrace floor and the soffit (Fig. 30–31).

While modern physical culture, like any facet of modern life, largely drew its appeal from the implicit promise of liberation from old ways of thinking, it seems to have manifested itself differently from one culture to the next. If Breuer, or Gropius for that matter, approached their experiments as practitioners of physical culture—and this seems entirely likely given the importance of physical culture at the Bauhaus, and in the Weimar Republic more generally—there's nothing in the careful implementation of their projects to suggest it.[40] Breuer, even in his House for a Sportsman, seems to have approached his task with almost scholarly focus, as a question of organization more so than of spirit, a problem to be solved rather than an opportunity to be explored.

The same could hardly be said of their French contemporaries. While the modest gymnasium implemented on the roof terrace of André Lurçat's Villa Guggenbühl, known also as the Hôtel Particulier (Fig. 32–33), completed in Paris in 1925, anticipated a number of comparable projects in Germany by several years, those who carried the torch forward in the years that followed did so with an altogether more euphoric sensibility. In 1927, Robert Mallet-Stevens completed the Villa Noailles in Hyères (Fig. 34–37), an extravagant cubist pleasure palace designed for a wealthy couple whose patronage of the arts placed them at the social epicenter of the French avant-garde during the interwar period.[41] Their circle included the likes of Coco Chanel, Jean Cocteau, and Man Ray, whose 1929 film *Les Mystères du Château de Dé* was partially set in the house. The film prominently featured the couple and their friends cavorting, in matching swimming suits, around a second-story terrace adjacent to an indoor swimming pool and a private gymnasium. Although one might reasonably assume from this example that physical culture represented something more hedonistic in France, it should also be observed that there is nothing here of the programmatic synthesis that made Breuer's projects so compelling. It would be Charlotte Perriand, then at the advent of her career, who would bridge the gap between the playful impulse of Mallet-Stevens' mansion and Breuer's experimental rigor, and in unforgettable fashion.

In 1929, Perriand published a series of drawings depicting two projects in the decorative arts magazine *Repertoire du Gout Moderne*. Perriand had designed these works, titled *Travail et Sport* and *Salle de Culture Physique* respectively, two years prior, in 1927 (Fig. 38–42). While these were designed in the same year that the Piscator apartment and the Villa Noailles were completed, Perriand's work was far more radical at this moment. There is a sense of freedom in these compositions, bordering on the ecstatic, that suggests an intuitive understanding of how physical culture could be integrated into domestic space. In *Travail et Sport*, the objects associated with physical culture—a free-standing punching bag, a wall-mounted archery target, a rack of fencing swords, monkey bars suspended from the ceiling, and wall bars doubly functioning as a ladder to a lofted hammock—are given equal consideration to the furniture, kitchen fixtures, and pedestal typewriter, all invariably of her own design.[42] Rather than arranging objects to define strict programmatic zones, Perriand intermingles them freely around a core of functional amenities (stovetop, storage, etc.). The effect is dynamic, lively, and playful, yet these compositions still exhibit remarkable precision.

Though we have only a single perspective by which to judge *Salle de Culture Physique*, it is characterized by many of the same strengths (and similar equipment) as the more developed *Travail et Sport*. Here, too, a free-standing, spring-loaded punching bag, wall-mounted archery target, and cantilevered monkey bars (extending from behind the field of view into the exaggerated depth of the room) coexist with novel modern furniture (notably a wall-mounted, apparently hideaway daybed which hints at the design she would make famous in the 1950s). In the center of a room is a free-standing, floor-mounted set of wall bars that doubles as a signpost indicating a swimming pool behind the viewer, and showers to the left. Taking these two projects as companion pieces and noting their shared affinity for deftly composing gymnastic apparatuses and furniture, it is not unreasonable to think that Perriand may have regarded these objects collectively as "domestic equipment," a turn of phrase widely credited to Le Corbusier to describe the iconic furniture Perriand went on to design under the auspices of his and Pierre Jeanerret's Paris atelier in the following decade, but which may just as well have sprung from her imagination.[43]

No doubt due to the enthusiastic reception these furniture designs met upon their release, Perriand went on to play an increasingly pivotal role in the atelier's output. Her input may have been the impetus for a growing visibility of physical culture in the works of Le Corbusier and Jeanneret during this period. She is, for example, noted as the primary designer of the Villa Martínez de Hoz (Fig. 43), a private house designed in 1930 for an affluent physician in Buenos Aires.[44] Much like her unrealized projects from *Repertoire du Gout Moderne*, this proposal was distinguished by a sequence of Perriand's charismatic perspective renderings. And though the organization and materiality depicted in the proposal suggest that Perriand may have consciously tailored her designs to fit more neatly into the continuity of previous free-standing houses by Le Corbusier and Jeanneret (the house registers as an exemplary manifestation of at least some of Le Corbusier's "Five Points"), she nonetheless found a way to place physical culture front and center. One of the most tantalizing renderings of the project is a rather exaggerated perspective of the roof terrace, equipped with a swimming pool and various pieces of gymnastic equipment (a punching bag and barbells sit in the foreground, while a set of wall bars is mounted against a wall in the far distance), all mediated by a lush cactus garden.

Five years later, Perriand (working alongside colleagues René Herbst and Louis Sognot) oversaw the conceptualization, design, and realization of the speculative *La maison du jeune homme* (House of a Young Man), the atelier's contribution to the Exposition Universelle in Brussels (Fig. 44–45). Installed at one-to-one scale, this project organized essential functions of a live-work space—a bathroom, twin bed, and modular wardrobe, as well as a studio equipped with wall-mounted shelving, a large desk with chairs, and a free-standing slate blackboard—into a roughly L-shaped configuration around a generous rectangular "courtyard," double-height and illuminated via a backlit fabric ceiling. Photographs of the exhibition clearly convey that this space was intended, above all, to serve as a gymnasium. Partitioned from the domestic perimeter by both a pair of sliding wooden doors on the "living" side, and a large wall of netting on the studio side, this space was equipped with an exhaustive collection of sporting equipment: a rowing machine, a floor-mounted punching bag (with several sets of boxing gloves hanging from a nearby hook), barbells and juggling pins, suspended climbing ropes and gymnastic rings, as well as a variety of balls (presumably the netting was intended to prevent these from wreaking havoc in the adjoining studio). In a manner comparable to Breuer's House for a Sportsman of four years prior, physical culture serves here as the impetus for a new vision of the domestic interior, offering an even more seductive glimpse at how modernism might yet transform the rituals of everyday life.

The intuitive feeling that Perriand demonstrates for this interplay of traditionally domestic objects and gymnastic equipment suggests greater familiarity with how these objects were used. This can likely be chalked up to the fact that physical culture was crucial to her own lifestyle. Perriand's living and working spaces frequently operated as testing grounds for ideas that would find their way into her designs.[45] In a photograph Perriand snapped of her own Montparnasse workshop in 1938, a pair of ceiling-mounted gymnastic rings hover in the foreground, so close by to her breakfast table that they could have been used to lift oneself from a sitting position (Fig. 46). Photographs of the architect from throughout her long career suggest a designer for whom modernism, broadly speaking, represented not merely an aesthetic preference, but an all-encompassing way of life. With regard to the arrival of the gymnasium in the modern home, Perriand seems to have gone well beyond a studied consideration of how a hypothetical *somebody* might inhabit such a hybridized space. Rather, we can surmise from the inclusion of such equipment in her own domestic environments that Perriand enjoyed a stronger, more intimate connection to physical culture than many contemporaries, which may account for the livelier, more playful tone of the projects examined here.

The integration of physical culture into the domestic sphere was also a central preoccupation in Italy during this period, though here it is somewhat more difficult to disentangle architectural thought, and indeed the notion of the modern body, from the political ideology of the moment. In Germany, most leading figures of the modern movement—Gropius, Breuer, Mies, and many more—fled over the course of the Nazis' drawn-out consolidation of power, leaving architecture to become dominated by a small coterie of architects whose dedication to the state-sponsored variety of monumental, stripped-back neoclassicism was beyond question. By contrast, the Italian avant-garde seem to have been given a seat at the table without any such preconditions. On its surface, the internationalist and experimental thrust of modern architecture might seem to conflict with the Fascist obsession with tradition and national identity. Upon closer inspection, however, the progressive spirit of the movement could be, and was, easily construed as sympathetic to the more technophilic leanings of Mussolini's government. The 1926 manifesto of Gruppo 7—an association of young rationalists that included the likes of Giuseppe Terragni, Luigi Figini, and Gino Pollini—painstakingly avoided framing their work in opposition to the tenets of the Fascist party that had assumed power only four years prior.

> "...This must be clear...we do not intend to break with tradition... The new architecture, the true architecture, should be the result of a close association between logic and rationality."[46]

Because this rhetorical and theoretical maneuvering successfully yielded a degree of acceptance by the Fascist state—and at times even its outright patronage—the Italian avant-garde actually flourished during this period.[47] Over time, this would feed into an unusual state-endorsed style that filtered references to classical materiality and ornament through the formal restraint of modernism.[48]

The fascination with the domestic potential of physical culture seems to have transcended political affiliation, even at this charged moment. Take, for example, the V Triennale di Milano of 1933, which included a series of experimental model houses, built to full scale in the Parco Sempione. Among these houses was a project entitled *Casa dell'aviatore*, or "House for an Aviator." The project was a result of the collaboration between three Friulian architects—Cesare Scoccimarro, Pietro Zanini, and Ermes Midena—whose very collaboration speaks to the range of personal political beliefs held by those practitioners who continued to operate during Mussolini's rule. The trio's relationship with the Fascist regime ranged from outright party membership in Midena's case to Scoccimarro's eventual involvement with the underground resistance following the Armistice of Cassibile in 1943.[49] Nonetheless, that the house was intended to accommodate an imaginary but explicitly martial inhabitant indicates the degree to which discourse surrounding the modern body in the country was dictated by the military regime.

Any tension generated by the designers' various political alignments is not ultimately legible in the House for an Aviator. At first glance, the house appears to be relatively normative for modern architecture of the period: a two-story, box-like arrangement of planes clad in white stucco. Only upon entering do we recognize the distinctive character of the house. In addition to the stylishly furnished but ultimately conventional kitchen and living area, the house included a gymnasium, not merely adjoining the bedroom but in fact part of it (Fig. 48–49). Photos from the exhibition demonstrate that apart from the bed itself, there was practically no furniture in this austere space. As with Perriand's unrealized projects or Breuer's Piscator apartment, the gymnastic equipment itself must therefore be understood as the furniture. Most conspicuously, a punching bag is suspended between the floor and ceiling steps from the foot of the bed; a rowing machine and wall bars are situated nearby. The association between physical culture and military pursuits, in this case obviously aviation, is made abundantly clear by the provision of a hangar on the ground floor, precisely dimensioned to house a small experimental aircraft with collapsible wings. Linking this hangar to the hybridized gymnasium and living quarters was the most unusual innovation in the house: a helix staircase, seemingly wrapped around a heavy cylindrical column, which in fact masked a vertical shaft with a sliding pole (Fig. 50). When called into action, the eponymous aviator could reach his aircraft in the blink of an eye, a singular moment of architecture as expression of physical culture.

Given that the House for an Aviator was envisioned for a burgeoning class of sophisticated military elites, it is a somewhat flawed measure for how the Italian avant-garde reconciled physical culture with a more recognizably domestic architecture. However, it would not be long before new case studies emerged. In fact, it would be the house of a leading Italian architect that demonstrated a more civilian fascination with bringing sport into the home. In 1934, Luigi Figini completed the construction of his house in Milan. While its white plaster facade and rectangular volume punctuated by ribbon windows wasn't uncharacteristic of modernist houses of the period (bearing a strong resemblance to Le Corbusier's early work, or that of fellow Grupo 7 founder Terragni), Figini set his house apart by dramatically elevating the building four meters above the street on twelve columns.[50] The ostensibly rationalist facade obscured an organization of spaces than was far from conventional: not only interiors but, crucially, a sequence of staggered open-air terraces at both the front and back of the house, amenities that very well may have been understood as the front and back "yards" if not for the house's otherworldly displacement from the ground plane.

The terraces are of special interest because of a handful of photographs taken not long after the house's completion. One of these depicts Gege Figini, wife of the architect, posing beside a set of gymnastic rings and a climbing rope, which are suspended from a concrete beam on the paved terrace on the top floor (Fig. 51). On the other end of the topmost floor, another terrace provided Figini's family with a diminutive "lawn," along with a small, shallow pool and hammock (Fig. 52).

By relegating these spaces of physical culture and leisure to an elevated terrace, Figini aligns his work more closely to that of Döcker or Effenberger than to the more adroit syntheses of Breuer or Perriand. On the other hand, as with Perriand's Montparnasse studio, this was Figini's own residence, a fact that naturally suggests physical culture may have been more internalized and authentic to his thinking.

Two years later, Franco Albini, then in the earliest stages of his career, produced a remarkable exhibition space for the VI Triennale di Milano of 1936, entitled "Room for a Man" (Fig. 53–56). Simultaneously intimate and austere, this atmospheric space served as an index accounting for the most indispensable needs of modern living, neatly articulating Albini's take on the German notion of *Existenzminimum*. The inclusion of a rowing machine, a gymnastic mat, and a storage area stocked with equipment for various outdoor sports (camping, climbing, and hiking) in the composition—which otherwise included an elevated bed, a curtain for dressing, an Albini-designed desk and chair for writing, a standing shower with shaving mirror, and a hand sink—clearly speaks to the importance physical culture had assumed in modernist thought. The room was divided into loosely defined zones by partitions composed of gridded metal or glass, separating the programs without impeding visibility or communication, as well as providing hanging storage. The glass partition between the desk and the area containing the gymnastic mat and "sporting locker" was adorned with diagrams Albini had drawn to illustrate a variety of basic calisthenic exercises.

While Scoccimarro, Zanini, and Midena's House for an Aviator allows us to see the creeping influence of militant rhetoric on the modern body, Albini's project echoed and built upon both Breuer's and Perriand's earlier, ideologically like-minded installations. The crucial difference? By 1936, physical culture was no longer understood as a mere amenity for a specialized inhabitant. What Breuer had once imagined for the *sportsman*, or Perriand and her colleagues for the *young man*, had become one of the few indispensable parts of modern domesticity for *every* man.[51]

The impact of physical culture on modern architecture was hardly limited to Europe. If the frenzy that had met the arrival of Delsarte's aesthetic gymnastics some fifty years earlier offered any indication, the United States was every bit as attuned to the appeal of this cult of the body. And indeed by the 1920s, health culture had blossomed into a full-fledged movement, most notably on the West Coast. In 1927, having emigrated from Vienna only four years prior, Richard Neutra was tapped to design the Los Angeles home of Philip Lovell, a well-known physician and naturopath, and his wife Leah (née Press), a teacher whose ideas about progressive education and natural living situated her as something of an ideological descendent of Rousseau, Basedow, and others.[52] Philip enjoyed enormous notoriety in Southern California as the writer of a popular column in the *Los Angeles Times*' Sunday magazine entitled "Care of the Body," in which he advocated for everything from sunbathing to vegetarianism with almost evangelical fervor. Promoting a range of cutting-edge, frequently controversial, but invariably natural remedies for all manner of health considerations, Lovell was one of the most visible proponents of physical culture in a city that would play a central role in defining a new standard of physical beauty for the 20th century.

True to character, the Lovells insisted on a new kind of house that would facilitate and embody their particular notions about healthy living. Neutra, recognizing the transformative significance of this opportunity, adopted a strategy for which he would become increasingly known over the course of his career, consulting with his clients in exhaustive detail in order to comprehend the unique requirements of their philosophy and lifestyle. Furthermore, in order to ensure the quality of the final construction, he opted to serve as both architect and contractor. The house was to be situated on steep hillside adjacent to Los Angeles' Griffith Park, a feature that Neutra went on to exploit to dazzling effect. Opting for a steel frame structure (often cited as the first of its kind in a domestic project in the United States), he freed himself to deploy large expanses of glass along the south-facing facade, ensuring that the clients could enjoy the healing rays of the sun as they flooded the interior at every level of the house. The inclusion of a sequence of terraces and patios ensured that the Lovells would also never be far from the outdoors, able to step outside at a moment's notice and at a variety of elevations. Neutra scattered a variety of health-oriented programs across these outdoor spaces—a swimming pool, of course, but also a "sleeping patio," and elsewhere a steel structure from which a variety of gymnastic rings, bars, and swings were suspended for the inhabitants' use in their various exercise regimens (Fig. 57–59).

The Lovell Health House was an immediate sensation in Los Angeles, aided in no small part by the effusive publicity the famous client heaped upon his architect. It would go on to be included in the Museum of Modern Art's "Modern Architecture: International Exhibition" in 1932, which set the terms for what became known as the International Style. The house also helped to establish a new agenda for West Coast modernism for the coming decades, one which Neutra, who came to view the Lovell house as a crucial inflection point in his career, would continue to develop in the flood of residential commissions that followed. Although Neutra had implemented them to serve the singular needs of his clients—that is, to facilitate a lifestyle defined by a sweeping embrace of physical culture in all of its facets—the strategies he used in the Lovell House would nonetheless come to influence a material, formal, and organizational vocabulary embraced by a rising generation of American architects and exemplified by the Case Study House program of the 1950s (in which Neutra himself would participate), though the inclusion of physical culture as an explicit programmatic consideration in these projects was curiously absent. It is precisely in this mid-century vocabulary that we find one of the most unmistakable examples of what we perceive to be a more general tendency in this period—that is, for the modern house to display, both materially and formally, a certain indebtedness to the tropes of the gymnasium.

In 1936, Neutra was commissioned to design a small house in Palm Springs for Grace Lee Miller, a devoted practitioner and instructor of Bess Mensendieck's method of functional gymnastics. Neutra is said to have accepted the commission explicitly because of his fascination with the Mensendieck method, going so far as to insist, upon the project's completion, that it be published as the "Mensendieck House," rather than under the client's name. The project (Fig. 60–63) has the distinction of being Neutra's first "desert house," the initial antecedent and, one might say, testing ground for many of the ideas that would subsequently be refined in the more canonical Kaufmann House ten years later. True to his reputation, the architect exchanged numerous letters with Miller from 1936 to 1937 to learn more about her lifestyle, as well as to better apprehend the minutiae of the Mensendieck method. This correspondence and spirit of collaboration provided Neutra with the insight to personalize many aspects of the house to a degree that many modern architects more preoccupied with standardization would likely never have attempted, and sharpened his understanding of the sort of space Miller would require to synthesize her individual needs with the practice and teaching of the Mensendieck system.

In contrast to many of the other projects already covered, Neutra seems to have been unconcerned with highlighting the synthesis of "house" and "dance studio" and—possibly driven to achieve a convincing neutrality—there is almost no distinction between the two programs at all. Photographs of the house during Miller's long inhabitation seem to support this conclusion. Perhaps this is because Mensendieck's method required none of the equipment that symbolized many of these others projects' alignment with the movement of physical culture. This freed Neutra to design with greater emphasis on continuity of space, as well as proportion and materiality. In this way, the Mensendieck House might be the most appropriate, though inadvertent, predecessor for understanding how the ambiguous spaces of the Villa Tugendhat would later be reinterpreted as a gymnasium. Only the more concentrated use of mirrored surfaces offers a clear indication of which area served as Miller's studio—the mirror was an indispensable accessory for practicing Mensendieck's method, used to assure that practitioners were performing the prescribed movements as meticulously as possible. Then again, Neutra's penchant for deploying mirrors liberally in his other projects brings the project into dialogue with the material vocabulary he developed over the duration of his career. There is little in terms of technique separating Neutra's use of the mirror in Miller's house from his subsequent uses, including in his own residence, the VDL Research House. The blurring of this line from the perspective of a contemporary, even well-versed observer—that is, between the use of the mirror as a functional element of a specialized, gymnastic program, and the use of the mirror because it is a *modern* material—is so thorough as to reinforce our instinct that for many advocates of modern architecture, at one point or another, the distinction simply ceased to matter.

—

To describe the Second World War as a period of upheaval for the modern movement seems somehow insufficient. Indeed, the war represented a schism so complete that it has been said that modernity, as an emancipatory social and political project, never totally recovered.[53] This moment of rupture is undeniable with regard to modern architecture, reflected in the dilution of our subjects' shared fascination with physical culture, as well as to their work to integrate it into the domestic sphere. The war was, in effect, the end of a conversation. Indeed, these projects were not conducted in isolation, but rather were a discursive phenomenon, each project building upon the discoveries of the last in order to achieve an ever more compelling challenge to what was possible in, or even crucial to, the formulation of the modern home. Perhaps the interruption of this discourse owes to the simple passage of time, to the rise of new fashions, or to a fascination with the potential of new technologies developed in the intervening years. It may have been cut short by the scattering of European modernism's leading figures to various corners of the globe—Gropius and Breuer to London and later Massachusetts, Mies to Chicago, Meyer to Moscow, Perriand to Japan, and so forth. Or perhaps it is a question of a more profound disillusionment with where their experiments had led. After all, despite having been framed in the most utopian terms possible during the Weimar years, the fact remains that the Nazis were able to appropriate the modern "cult of the body" with remarkable ease, perverting physical culture into a popular representation of their central Aryan myth. In all likelihood, it was a combination of all of these factors. Whatever the case may be, when the fog of war lifted in 1945, physical culture—or at any rate the *program* of physical culture—was conspicuously absent from even the most experimental domestic architecture that followed.[54]

But while the disappearance of the wall bars, rowing machines, punching bags, and other explicit object signifiers of physical culture from domestic space certainly represents a conclusion to a crucial chapter of our story, we are left with the unshakable impression that modern domestic architecture has been haunted, in a manner of speaking, by these projects. The spatial configurations and material vocabulary that were developed during those years, techniques which had so sharply characterized efforts to integrate the gymnasium into the modern home, proliferated across the postwar architectural field, even as the objective itself ceased to be a driving concern. The emphatic repetition of these gestures was such that they could often be perceived as signaling toward a missing *something*, and yet, deprived of their intended discursive and functional clarity, they instead produced only ambiguity. The progression of postwar modern architecture strikes us as increasingly littered with forms that seem to frame or contain some mysterious, invisible apparatus, an impression that can likely be traced to this moment of retreat. But equally pronounced was the uncertainty with which prewar modern projects were interpreted as they were gradually rediscovered and discussed anew in the decades that followed.

This ambiguity returns us to the peculiar resuscitation of the Villa Tugendhat, an unlikely culmination of this narrative, and yet one which is all the more potent for its lack of clear relation to the other projects. In contrast to many of his contemporaries, there is nothing in the work to suggest that Mies was especially enamored with physical culture.[55] In any case, this house, designed for a couple with young children, certainly wouldn't have been the ideal venue for him to explore these themes. What sets the house apart from other projects of the period was not the introduction of new wrinkles to the domestic program so much as the architecture itself: peculiarities in the plan that suggest a certain irreverence for the old conventions of domestic organization, particularly those concerned with circulation and the separation of "public" and "private" regions of the house. Julius Posener observed that the route taken by guests cuts directly across the path connecting the bedrooms from the living area, a gesture that would likely have been considered shocking only a few years earlier.[56] Similarly, Jean-Louis Cohen has written that the organization of the bedrooms along a corridor gives the impression of "first-class cabins on a transatlantic liner."[57] Without furniture, however, they might just as easily signify offices, studios, or indeed the examination rooms they became during the house's years as a physical therapy clinic.

Then there is the conspicuous question of the house's spaciousness, which, coupled with the luxuriousness of the original materials (ebony, travertine, onyx, chromed steel, "milk glass") was deemed by some critics at the time to be ostentatious at best, and heretical at worst. The materials and forms in the house clearly call to mind those of Mies's German Pavilion in Barcelona, which preceded the Tugendhat so narrowly that it was still under construction at the time that he broke ground in Brno. The projects are siblings, in a manner of speaking, and together represent the crystallization of Mies's particular attitude towards materiality during one of the most remarkable phases of his career. And while the echo of the Pavilion was so unmistakable as to prompt *Die Form* to dismiss the house as "exhibition architecture," isn't it precisely this luxury, this scale, this lack of the familiar warmth typical of an older form of domestic architecture, that allowed the house to be so easily adapted to a different use in the years after the war?[58] The radicality of Mies's design rendered the house a site of programmatic ambiguity, and the people of Brno, in a wonderful historical twist, recognized only a space ideally suited to the cultivation of the modern body.

—

The striking resonance between the Villa Tugendhat and the German Pavilion, along with the photographs that emerged from Miloš Budík's visit to Brno in 1956, were clearly very much on Rem Koolhaas's mind thirty years later. For the 1986 Triennale di Milano, Koolhaas's Office for Metropolitan Architecture received a semi-circular fragment of the Palazzo dell'Arte. The first of three successive phases of the Triennale, the exhibition was dedicated to the question of "The Domestic Project." Koolhaas responded to this provocation by reimagining Mies's German Pavilion, contorting it to conform to the curvature of his allotted space. Dubbed *La Casa Palestra*, or "home gymnasium," the project was accompanied by a mythic (and utterly engrossing) "history" detailing the pavilion's fate after the conclusion of the International Exposition—its brief stint as headquarters for an anarchist organization during the Spanish Civil War; its piecemeal return to Berlin; the reappropriation of its marble surfaces as a backdrop for a Third Reich propaganda film; and its repurposing after the Allied victory, first as a military hospital, then a social club, and finally a locker room for the doomed 1952 Olympic Games. All this, of course, was dreamt up by Koolhaas, a former screenwriter, who had from OMA's earliest days demonstrated a sharp understanding of the flimsiness of history—and the eagerness with which alternate narratives, suitably seductive, will be devoured as fact. It is no coincidence that Koolhaas selected the German Pavilion as his instrument of transgression. The alternate-reality misadventures of the Casa Palestra may have been intended, at least in part, to critique the pavilion's painstaking reconstruction by Ignasi de Solá-Morales, Christian Cirici, and Fernando Ramos, then underway in Barcelona. It would be as if the pavilion had never budged, a gesture Koolhaas seems to have understood as a surreal negation of its decades-long absence—the erasure of erasure.

Drawing on the material similarities to the Villa Tugendhat, Koolhaas cleverly interpreted the German Pavilion as a multivalent space—simultaneously a house, a gymnasium, a *stage*—insinuating that, contrary to the typical understanding that these programs are distinct or incompatible, they are in fact inextricable within the framework of modernity. Performances throughout the duration of the Triennale especially evoked the space's fictional tenure as an Olympic locker room, the most explicit nod to Tugendhat's postwar fate and by extension the subliminal inscription of physical culture in Mies's vocabulary during that period. Photos of the exhibition depict dancers writhing across imitation travertine floors, contorting their bodies, or draping themselves sullenly over antique gymnastic equipment (Fig. 65–68).

Koolhaas used the occasion to observe that modern architecture was never the drab, moralizing force that many advocates of a then-fashionable architectural postmodernism (including many of his neighbors in the exhibition) claimed it to be.

"Recent attacks on modern architecture have described it as lifeless, empty, puritanical. However, it has always been our conviction that modern architecture is a hedonistic movement, that its abstraction, rigour and severity are in fact plots to create the most provocative settings for the experiment that is modern life."[59]

We would take this line of thinking even further. Detractors of modern architecture have continually leveled the criticism that the stripping of ornament and preoccupation with functionality characteristic of many projects of the 1920s and '30s fundamentally *limited* the ways in which it might be interpreted or occupied, that they seemed formulated to produce a particular outcome, an oppressively specific idea of the modern subject. But this interpretation is not only laughably cynical, it is also ironically reductive in its estimation of what forms of expression were achievable (and indeed *achieved*) within a framework that, as we have described, produced spaces of profound and fertile ambiguity. The modern project was, at its heart, the rejection of a code of cultural values inherited from a preceding generation that had, in the modernist view, marched humanity to the very brink of destruction in the First World War. The central task of modern architecture, therefore, was both to insist on a more optimistic use of the industrial technology that had been weaponized in that war, and to extricate the discipline from the societal role it had played up to that point—that is, expressing (and therefore fortifying) the aesthetic signifiers of a failed cultural premise. The assertion that architecture could be a functional language, with a central importance placed upon the democratizing potential of industrial methods of construction and the inherent value of practical materials, was ultimately devised to level the economic and cultural playing field, as well as to generate an aesthetic *tabula rasa* (or more appropriately, an unadorned, probably white wall) onto which new symbols, new programs, new identities, new *ways of life* could be projected.[60] In short, to offer a chance at *the good life* to the whole of a society disillusioned with and often traumatized by a then recent past.[61]

—

The broader modern movement, and the roles that architecture and physical culture in particular played within it, are far from uncomplicated. Any contemporary reading of the modern project cannot help but be colored by the recognition of its historical contradictions, including (but not limited to) the disturbing ease with which it has sometimes been appropriated by a more cynical and divisive politics.[62] As we have already acknowledged with regard to our own subjects, there is the question of an embedded ableism, sexism, and racism that accompanied modernism's assumptions about standardization and mass production, an insidious byproduct of the era in which it was formulated that nonetheless undercuts the credibility of any modernist claim to universality. Despite the utopian optimism underpinning both physical culture and the ostensibly functionalist architecture of the interwar period, they neglected to directly and emphatically embrace the incredible diversity of the human body, omitting and ostracizing, to varying degrees, women, people of color, those with disabilities, those who challenged notions of identity and gender, and others. Finally, the undeniably Eurocentric bent of the modern canon has produced a growing interpretation of both modern architecture and prevailing notions of physical beauty as aesthetic vestiges of colonialism. While this critique is certainly warranted with consideration to the latter, it is somewhat more complicated with regard to the former. A predictable insistence on the corrosive and totalizing effects of modern architecture on culture has often been accompanied by a failure to recognize the liberating, democratizing possibilities, or the potential for resistance, it was originally intended to (and on some occasions did) produce.

We are not blind to these complexities. Our work has frequently left us grappling with the same doubts that almost certainly dissuaded Breuer, Perriand, Albini, and others from continuing their experiments with the same intensity and directness in the aftermath of the war. We have struggled with the question of whether a critical reclamation of this fragment of the modern project is possible, or indeed appropriate. And yet, in spite of these questions—maybe, to some degree, even *because* of them—we remain captivated by these projects, in all of their palpable exuberance and unresolved potential. We are fascinated by them precisely because they were experiments, imperfect but daring non-sequiturs, perhaps deemed too quaint or unusual, and therefore rarely mentioned in discussions of the frequently canonical repertoires of their authors. In our estimation, it is precisely this incorporation of physical culture, a movement that had theretofore been understood as a pursuit for the masses, that these architects most effectively challenged prevailing notions of domestic space—how it looked, how it was organized, and perhaps most transformatively, what we do after we closed the door and find ourselves *at home*. These unassuming works suggest that at some intrinsic level, our protagonists may have recognized a tantalizing possibility, one that we believe is as crucially relevant to our present moment as it was a century ago, if not more so: that the individual and the collective do not operate, and indeed never have operated in dialectical opposition to one another. That by setting aside inherited, often moralistic notions of *the domestic sphere*, we render it possible to contribute to the collective project of producing a more equal and just society at the most intimate possible scale, the home. Though it may seem grand to make such a claim of physical culture—of *working out*, as we now conceive of it—the fact of the matter is that the arrival of the gymnasium in the modern house was quietly revolutionary. It suggests, however gently, that the central task of the dwelling is to provide the conditions for a profound act of self-invention, or perhaps more accurately, *self-construction*. At its most radical, this act can challenge archetypal ideas of identity, and thereby expand the scope of *who* constitutes that society.[63]

The projects collected here attempted to provide a framework for one of the most crucial aspects of this self-construction: the cultivation and expression of the modern body. We've grown to understand this phrase in a way that is both more expansive and responsive than it was understood to be a century ago. For us, the modern body represents agency. By this reasoning, the body of Jahn's militant and nationalistic *turner* was never modern, nor was the white, "typical" body codified by Neufert, nor even the normative female body shaped by the postures of the Mensendieck system, inspired as they were by the movements of quotidian domestic rituals. We assert that the modern body does not suggest a specific outcome. Rather, we interpret this phrase as pointing towards a more expansive and therefore potent field of possible ways of being, bound not by social constraints, but by instinct and imagination. In this formulation, the meeting of physical culture with domestic space, to say nothing of the programmatic ambiguity of the resulting spaces, were then, and remain now, essential to making this act of self-construction possible. It opened the door for the understanding that domestic space need not be understood as strictly private. On the contrary, the home gymnasium expanded and modernized "the domestic" in such a way as to connect even an isolated inhabitant to a more collective project. Alone, but always together.

For us, it is precisely this more expansive interpretation of the modern body that has come to constitute the substance and promise of *the advanced school of collective feeling*, a phrase with implications that for us stretch far beyond Meyer's acknowledgment of a burgeoning mass culture. It is our conviction that the humanist thrust of the modern movement supersedes its admittedly flawed claims to universality, and must be recognized for having dramatically expanded the scope of our collective understanding of *whose* world it is we ought to be building.

It is true that architects have slavishly recreated the white walls, vast expanses of glass, and other gestures that became the aesthetic signifiers of modern architecture. This complacency allowed a genuinely radical movement to ossify, to become a mere idiom, a *style* ironically devoid of the critical reflection that was always intended to accompany the implementation, habitation, and indeed the broader performance of modern life. At its very worst, the language of modern architecture, coupled with an acritical faith in the merit of technology, has served as a herald for unbridled development, resuscitating or amplifying crises the original movement was largely formulated to mitigate. We would argue that the deployment of these techniques to such disastrous ends are a perversion of the word *modern*.

So, we are not advocating for some empty, purely aesthetic modern revival. Far from it. Rather, we are more concerned with an acknowledgment of the continued relevance and unresolved possibility of a genuinely transformative mode of thinking, one that flourished all too briefly. To understand that while it fully deserves to be questioned, reconsidered, and indeed *redesigned* to embrace those who continue to feel alienated by the shortcomings of the modern movement as it played out a century ago, we are nonetheless living in a moment in which this particular way of relating both to ourselves and to one another still holds enormous potential. This expanded notion of *collective feeling* may therefore still offer the basis for an architecture for our own times. A modern architecture rooted in this thinking ought not be understood as some vacuous style, nor as an unassailable gospel. It was not conceived, as modern architecture more generally has often been accused, by and for a privileged few. Rather, it was intended to free people of the expectations of the past, to enable new forms of expression, to hammer away at the boundaries of what we can do and who we can choose to be. In short, to lay the groundwork for cultural revolution—a proposition that now, as was the case then, is not only necessary, but exhilarating.

1. Budík's photos suggest that only one of the original panes of monolithic glass survived by the time of his visit in 1956.
2. Frequently used in that period as a patching or subfloor material, xylolite is a composite material consisting of sawdust and Sorel cement. Throughout this room's tenure as a space of physical culture (nearly thirty-five years, a rather lengthy chapter in the house's history) and right up until the first attempt to restore the house to its original state in the early 1980s, this bright red floor treatment rendered this most iconic of Miesian spaces into something altogether different. The floor would undoubtedly have been one of the most memorable aspects of the room, emblazoned in the memories of generations of young people who exercised there, and inextricable from the still extant onyx wall and chrome columns. Though Budík's black-and-white photos could not convey these qualities, the room would be photographed again in 1968 by the German architect Peter Zerweck, this time in color. For a more detailed account of the renovation, see Iveta Černá and Dagmar Černoušková's *Mies in Brno. Tugendhat House* (2018). We are indebted to Barbora Benčíková from the Villa Tugendhat for her invaluable help in better understanding these alterations and materials.
3. Rousseau, Jean-Jacques. *Emile: or On Education*. Translated by Allan Bloom. New York: Basic Books, (1763) 1979. 118.
4. Whereas *sport* derives from the Old French *desport*, meaning "leisure," *gymnastics* traces its origins to the Greek *gymnastikos*, meaning "fond of or skilled in bodily exercise." So, it might be said that *gymnastics* is the crucial precursor to these other terms and the philosophies that accompanied them with regard to the cultivation of the body.
5. Needless to say, there are exceptions. The influence of the ancient Greeks on the formulation of Enlightenment ideals was pervasive, and predictably enough the athletic culture of ancient Greece was frequently cited as inspiration for the gymnastics movements of the 18th and 19th centuries, most conspicuously Pierre de Coubertin's resurrection of the Olympic Games in 1894.
6. Rousseau, 125.
7. Kant, Immanuel and E.F. Buchner. *The Educational Theory of Immanuel Kant*. Philadelphia & London: J.B. Lippincott Co., 1908. 242–246.
8. Quick, Robert Herbert. *Essays on Educational Reformers*. New York: E.L. Kellogg and Co, 1890. 144–162.
9. Basedow, straining under the pressure of ongoing conflict with his own faculty, resigned from the directorship of the school in 1778. The Philanthropinum continued under new leadership until its eventual dissolution in 1793.
10. Lempa, Heikki. *Beyond the Gymnasium: Educating the Middle-class Bodies in Classical Germany*. Plymouth: Lexington Books, 2007. 73–76.
11. Naul, Roland. *Olympic Education*. Maidenhead: Meyer and Meyer, 2008. 40–42.
12. Baker, William Joseph. *Sports in the Western World*. Urbana: University of Illinois Press, 1988. 100.
13. Ibid.
14. Ibid.
15. Ibid.
16. Melnick, Samantha. "Per Henrik Ling: Pioneer of Physiotherapy and Gymnastics," in *The European Journal of Physical Education and Sports Science*, Vol. 1, Issue 1, 2015.
17. Jahn is remembered today in Germany as the "father of gymnastics," probably to denote his expansion on the principles established by GutsMuths, who is likewise commemorated as the "grandfather."
18. Mosse, George L. *The Image of Man: The Creation of Modern Masculinity*. New York: Oxford University Press, 2010. 43–45.
19. Kyle, Donald G. and Gary D. Stark, Eds. *Essays on Sport History and Sport Mythology*. College Station: Texas A&M Press, 1990. 121–123.

20 Jahn is sporadically credited for either inventing or popularizing numerous devices which remain ubiquitous in gymnastics to this day, including the pommel horse, gymnastic rings, and both the horizontal and parallel bars.

21 "What was original, convincing, and imitable about Jahn's physical education was that it was a designed amalgam of patriotism, community-reinforcing festivities, and exuberant bodily activities. To conservative opponents of revolutionary patriotism, Jahn's program looked dangerous—and it was." Kyle and Stark, 121–123.

22 Kyle and Stark, 121–123.

23 For a thorough account of these phenomena, including how the Third Reich would ultimately appropriate physical culture in the aftermath of the Weimar Republic, see Georges Teyssot's "Figuring the Invisible" from *A Topology of Everyday Constellations* (Cambridge, MA: MIT Press, 2013).

24 Delsarte's preoccupation with "emotional truth" in performance brings a moralizing dimension to his philosophy, closely echoing the Rousseauian fixation on character that underpinned the work of every other progenitor of physical culture covered here. Perhaps not surprisingly, his students included numerous priests, some of whom supposedly advocated for his teachings to their congregations.

25 Delsarte's observations about human anatomy, frequently conveyed during his instruction, were so sharp that he was credited with the discovery that human beings curl their thumbs inward after death, a realization that led to more efficient rescue efforts by French authorities. This observation won Delsarte the admiration of the scientific community. He even delivered a lecture at the Faculty of Medicine in Paris in 1861.

26 Fischer, Iris Smith. "The role of séméiotique in François Delsarte's aesthetics." *Semiotica: Journal of the International Association for Semiotic Studies* 2018, no. 221 (February 2018): 123–142. doi.org/10.1515/sem-2015-0153.

27 Ibid.

28 Ibid.

29 Ibid.

30 "The New World" by Hannes Meyer. Original transcript from *Das Werk: Architektur und Kunst*, vol. 13 no. 7 (1926). English translation found in *The Weimar Republic Sourcebook* by Anton Kaes, Martin Jay, and Edward Dimendberg. Berkley: University of California Press, 1995. 445–450.

31 It is no coincidence that Mensendieck's method was frequently described in similar terms to Delsarte's system, i.e. "functional gymnastics" or "aesthetic gymnastics." Mensendieck studied under Genevieve Stebbins in the United States, and the influence of the latter's faithful interpretation of Delsarte's system on the formulation of Mensendieck's pedagogy is unmistakable. Toepfer, Karl. *Empire of Ecstasy: Nudity and Movement in German Body Culture*, 1910–1935. Berkeley: University of California Press, 1997. 41.

32 Meyer's inclusion of Palucca in this observation about the importance of sport (and the stadium in particular) to the emergence of mass culture was prescient, if somewhat ironic. Following the Nazis' consolidation of power in 1933, Palucca was forced to hide her Jewish lineage, and eventually induced to close her dance school. In spite of this, she accepted an invitation to serve as one of the choreographers of the "mass games" style spectacles during the opening ceremony of the 1936 Olympic Games in Berlin.

33 While we are repeating this phrase quite intentionally to draw a link between Meyer's ideas about physical culture's role in mass culture and Jahn's work, we've found nothing to suggest that Meyer was familiar with Jahn's biography.

34 Granted, this phrase, the first translation we encountered, may be clumsy or even incorrect when held up against Meyer's intended meaning, but it is incredibly

evocative, so much so that it's served as the working title for this body of research from the earliest stages. It felt inevitable that it must serve as the title of this book.

35. By the time of Meyer's appointment as director, physical culture had already become one of the central fascinations of the Bauhauslers, and the student body in particular. The enthusiasm for sport was amply captured in T. Lux Feininger's iconic 1927 photograph "The Jump Over the Bauhaus" (Fig. 16). This enthusiasm continued for the duration of the school's existence, as evidenced by another set of photos by Feininger from 1930, this time documenting an afternoon gymnastics class on the roof terrace of the Prellerhaus (the school's dormitory block) led by Karla Grosch, a former student of Gret Palucca who had arrived in Dessau in 1928 to oversee the women's physical education course (Fig. 17–19).

36. "1. sex life, 2. sleeping habits, 3. pets, 4. gardening, 5. personal hygiene, 6. protection against weather, 7. hygiene in the home, 8. car maintenance, 9. cooking, 10. heating. 11. insolation, 12. service: these are the only requirements to be considered when building a house." Translated from the German by D.Q. Stephenson. From *Hannes Meyer, Buildings, Projects, and Writings*.

37. Given the Bauhaus founder's mentorship of Breuer, it bears speculating that the Piscator project could have come about due to Gropius's recommendation.

38. Unfortunately, our efforts to locate the architectural drawings of this project met a complete dead-end. Given that the commission arrived at such an early phase of his career, Breuer might not have archived his work as fastidiously as he would later on. In any case, we must assume the plans do not survive.

39. Naturally, one might question whether the inclusion of the gymnasium was at the insistence of the clients—the Piscators, and Erwin especially, being among the most influential figures in modern theater, a sphere that would have been impossible to separate from dance and therefore physical culture—or the suggestion of the young architect, who would doubtless have become familiar with the most current developments in physical culture during his time at the Bauhaus.

40. Breuer is, not coincidentally, one of our cover models. The illustration that graces the cover of this book is based on a 1921 photograph of Bauhaus students and faculty, including Laszlo Moholy-Nagy, Herbert Bayer, and others, forming a human pyramid during a trip to the beach.

41. The clients, Charles and Anne Marie de Noailles, are rumored to have interviewed both Mies van der Rohe and Le Corbusier for the project before settling on Mallet-Stevens, whose style better appealed to their artistic leanings.

42. Interestingly, Perriand's project suggests an embrace of explicitly martial sports—fencing, archery, boxing—more so than any other project we investigated. Yet it manages to do so in a way that feels playful, irreverent, and even a bit surreal.

43. Some of the furniture designs Perriand first projected for *"Travail et Sport"* would be realized the following year, albeit in slightly more developed form, as part of her contribution to the 1928 Salon des artistes Décorateurs exhibition in Paris. This includes a tubular steel chair with rotating seat and leather-padded back, an apparent synthesis of two designs that clearly appear in her taxonomy of furniture from the 1927 project. By the time of the 1928 Paris exhibition, Perriand had already been enlisted by Le Corbusier (in a reversal of his notoriously misogynistic dismissal of Perriand's application to work in his atelier, i.e. "we don't embroider cushions here."). Though designed prior to her collaboration with Le Corbusier, he nonetheless put Perriand's chair into mass production as the LC7—with himself and his cousin Pierre Jeanneret credited as co-authors of the design.

44 Thought to have remained unbuilt for decades, the house was completed some sixty years later by Argentinian architects who were purportedly unaware of the origin or author of the plans they had implemented. Barsac, Jacques. *Charlotte Perriand: Complete Works*. Zurich: Scheidegger & Spiess, 2014. 186–87.

45 It is no coincidence that her Bar Sous le Toit (Bar Under the Roof) at the 1927 Salon d'Automne, the design that launched her career, was realized in her own diminutive attic apartment.

46 Frampton, Kenneth. *Modern Architecture: A Critical History*. London: Thames & Hudson, 2010. 203.

47 The initial breadth of architectural possibility within the milieu of Fascist Italy, the perceived freedom to experiment, theorize, and critique, became more constrained and complicated over time, leading numerous architects who initially attempted to operate within the ideological framework of the regime to join the opposition, some going so far as to take up arms. The most notable example is probably Giuseppe Pagano, editor of *Casabella*, designer of another of the model homes for the 1933 Triennale di Milano, and organizer of the subsequent Triennale in 1936. While he initially supported the regime's agenda and enjoyed a prominent position in the architectural community under Mussolini, Pagano gradually became disillusioned with the party, using his platform to critique the restriction of cultural expression, and broke ranks entirely with the Fascist Party in 1942. He fought against the regime as a partisan, and was captured the following year, imprisoned and tortured. Pagano died in the Mauthausen concentration camp in Upper Austria in 1945.

48 In fact, the Fascist interpretation of physical culture would be expressed in one of the most iconic works in this style, Luigi Moretti's extravagant Palestra del Duce (Fig. 47), built as part of the Foro Italico from 1936 to 1937. This decadent complex, rendered almost entirely in marble, embellished with rich tapestries and furnished with modern furniture, blended the monumentality and materials of classicism with the formal and organizational abstraction of modernism. Gymnastic rings, punching bags, climbing ropes, and other equipment are suspended from impossibly high ceilings, while replicas of classical Roman statues overlooking the gymnasium served to remind users of a mythologized, nationalistic standard for which to strive.

49 Cesare came by his opposition to the Fascist regime honestly—he was the younger brother of Mauro Scoccimarro, a leading Italian socialist who had been exiled for his anti-Fascist activities.

50 The effect produced by the proportions of the house, the severity of its separation from the ground, its multitude of delicate columns, is (to state the obvious) to lend it an animal-like or even monstrous quality, not unlike that of John Hejduk's Berlin Masque and Victims projects a half-century later. One has the sense that, if you blink your eyes, Figini's house might just walk away.

51 True to the failings of discourse in this period, the idea that his functionalist scheme might just as easily be inhabited by a woman seems to have been troublingly removed from Albini's thinking.

52 Kilston, Lyra. *Sun Seekers: The Cure of California*. Edited by Ananda Pellerin. Los Angeles, CA: Atelier Editions, 2019.

53 Here we are thinking especially of Jürgen Habermas, who has described modernity as an "unfinished project," defending its emancipatory, utopian potential in the face of mounting skepticism in postwar intellectual circles.

54 There are a handful of exceptions. In 1953, Marcel Breuer produced a full-scale mock-up of a "Bathroom of the Future" (Fig. 64) for the U.S. State Department for possible inclusion in a consulate project. Breuer's design included the provision of a rowing machine and a ceiling-mounted

punching bag alongside more typical bathroom amenities.

55 Though Mies's absence from the interwar conversation about the "cult of the body" was conspicuous given his stature in the German scene, he did realize one project during this period that directly addressed the burgeoning importance of physical culture. In 1924, Mies completed a gymnasium on the grounds of a small private school in Potsdam. Curiously, though its proportions and rhythm of apertures are unsurprisingly elegant and its approach to space characteristically uncluttered, it nonetheless bears little resemblance to the refined modernism for which Mies would shortly be acknowledged as one of the movement's most essential champions. Though completed in the same year that the shifting planes of his unrealized Brick Country House were exhibited at the Novembergruppe exhibition, and only four years before the triumph of the Barcelona Pavilion, the gymnasium in Potsdam somehow owed far more to the neoclassical work of Schinkel than to Wright's Wasmuth portfolio (which famously galvanized a generation of German modernists when it was published in 1911).
56 Cohen, Jean-Louis. *Mies van der Rohe*. London: E. & F.N. Spon, 1996. 56–63.
57 Ibid.
58 Ibid.
59 Koolhaas, Rem / OMA. "La casa palestra." *AA Files*, no.13 (1987): 8–12.
60 And it was. We shouldn't forget that the same cultural milieu that produced the Bauhaus and the Weissenhof Estate—each built around the notion that the democratization of design produced greater economic equality—was also characterized by progressive social attitudes towards gender and sexuality that were brutally stamped out following the Nazis' rise to power.
61 To repurpose a phrase from the excellent book by Iñaki Ábalos.
62 We would argue that aesthetics more broadly, whether with regard to architecture or to the body, are inherently vulnerable to such appropriation, rather than owing to some specific quality of the modern movement.
63 Invoking this dichotomy is not intended as some rhetorical exercise. Rather, as we confront urgent, intertwining crises—deepening economic inequality, environmental devastation, assaults on human rights, and the renewed specters of nationalism and authoritarianism—we believe the question of the interrelation between social and political work, and the more familiar (to architects, anyway), seemingly abstract question of "how we live" remains paramount to any possible imagining of lasting solutions.

Fig. 1–7 The Villa Tugendhat was repurposed in the aftermath of the Second World War, first as a dance school and later a spinal rehabilitation clinic for the local children's hospital. The latter period was evocatively documented by photographer Miloš Budík in 1956.

Fig. 3

Fig. 5-6

Fig. 7

Fig. 8 An etching of an early gymnasium from *Gymnastik für die Jugend* (Gymnastics for the Youth), the seminal textbook by Johann Christoph Friedrich GutsMuths, first published in 1792.

Fig. 9–11　Swedish gymnastics at the Gymnastiska Centralinstitutet (Royal Gymnastics Central Institute) in Stockholm, around 1900.

Fig. 10

Fig. 11

Fig. 12 Friedrich Jahn's outdoor Turnplatz in Berlin was an early precedent for the modern gymnasium, as well as a hotbed of political activity.

Fig. 13 Women participating in a group exercise using the Mensendieck system of functional gymnastics in Oslo, Norway, 1950s.

Fig. 14　One of the premier innovators of modern dance in Weimar Germany, Gret Palucca's unconventional methods led to a close association with the Bauhaus. Not surprisingly, she is counted among the figures at the forefront of physical culture mentioned in Hannes Meyer's 1926 essay "Die Neue Welt."

Fig. 15 The gymnasium of the ADGB Trade Union School in Bernau-bei-Berlin, designed by Hannes Meyer and Hans Wittwer, 1928–30.

Fig. 16 Sport played an important role at the Bauhaus, bringing students, and occasionally teachers, together in a spirit of friendly competition and release. Here, students vie for control of a football in T. Lux Feininger's iconic photo, "The Jump Over the Bauhaus."

Fig. 17–19 Karla Grosch leading Bauhauslers through a gymnastics regimen atop the Prellerhaus, 1929.

Fig. 18–19

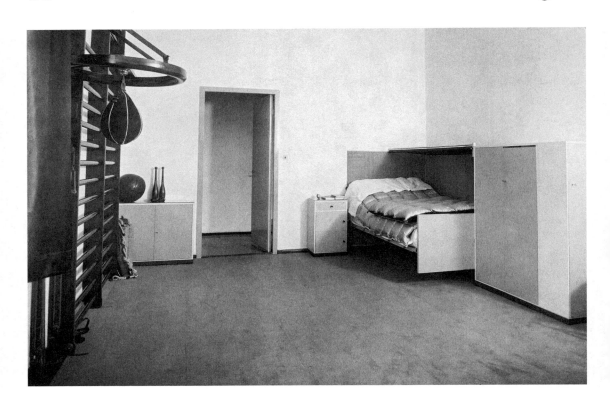

Fig. 20–21 Designed for Erwin and Hildegard Piscator, major figures in Berlin's avant garde theater scene, the apartment was one of Marcel Breuer's first architectural commissions after graduating from the Bauhaus. The project is most striking for the inclusion of a compact gymnasium in the bedroom. Destroyed during the Second World War, no drawings survived.

Fig. 21

Fig. 22 Breuer further developed his interest in integrating physical culture and domestic architecture with this compact but elegant apartment for gymnastics teacher Hilde Levi. The living spaces were cleverly organized to occupy roughly half of the apartment, making room for a generous gymnastics studio demarcated by a descending step and collapsible screen, and rubber wall paneling. Destroyed during the Second World War.

Fig. 23–25　Breuer's ongoing interest in this theme was most developed for his contribution to the 1931 Bauausstellung (Building Expo), the so-called House for a Sportsman. In this project, sport became the central focus of a domestic program.

Fig. 24

Fig. 25

Fig. 26–27 Breuer and Walter Gropius, along with fellow Bauhausler Herbert Bayer, included several pieces of gymnastic equipment in their Werkbund Exhibition at the 1930 Paris Expo.

Fig. 27

Fig. 28   Also for the 1931 Bauausstellung, Gropius proposed a series of shared amenities for the ground floor of his proposed high-rise housing project. These "communal rooms" were built for the exhibition, and included a gymnasium, swimming pool, and lounging area.

Fig. 29 For House 22, his contribution to the iconic Weissenhof Estate, Richard Döcker included a small terrace intended for exercise. A few years later, this image of a young woman exercising with a set of wall bars was included in his 1930 book, *Terrassen Typ*.

Fig. 30–31　Perhaps inspired by Docker's work in Stuttgart, Theo Effenberger included a similar provision for House 26/27, his contribution to the Deutscher Werkbund's WuWA Estate in Breslau (now Wrocław, Poland).

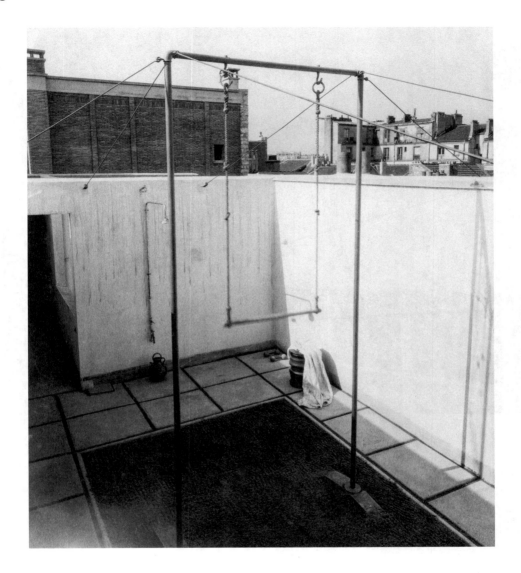

Fig. 32–33   In Paris, André Lurçat included the provision of a set of gymnastic bars on the rooftop terrace of the Villa Guggenbühl (also known as the Hôtel Particulier), designed for the Swiss painter Walter Guggenbühl.

Fig. 33

Fig. 34–37 Commissioned by a wealthy couple with avant-garde leanings, the sprawling Villa Noailles dedicated significant space to physical culture. Robert Mallet-Stevens provided his clients with both a large indoor swimming pool and a compact but well-outfitted gymnasium, joined together by a large third-floor terrace for sunbathing and exercise.

Fig. 35–36

Fig. 37

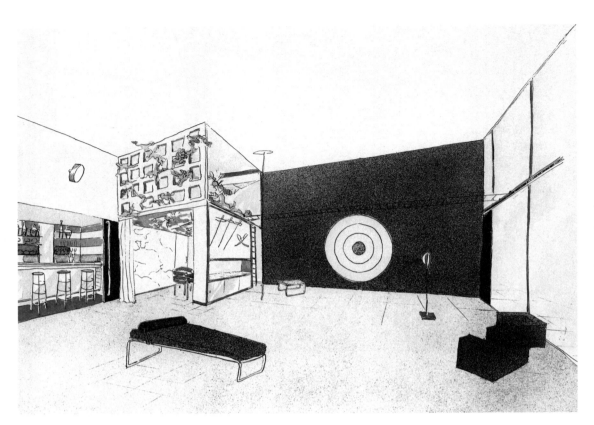

Fig. 38–42   Designed in 1927 but published two years later in the decorative arts journal *Repertoire du Gout Moderne*, Charlotte Perriand's radical, unrealized projects Travail et Sport and Salle de Culture Physique demonstrate a clear ambition to integrate the trappings of physical culture into the home, where they would mingle freely with her modern take on "domestic equipment."

Fig. 39

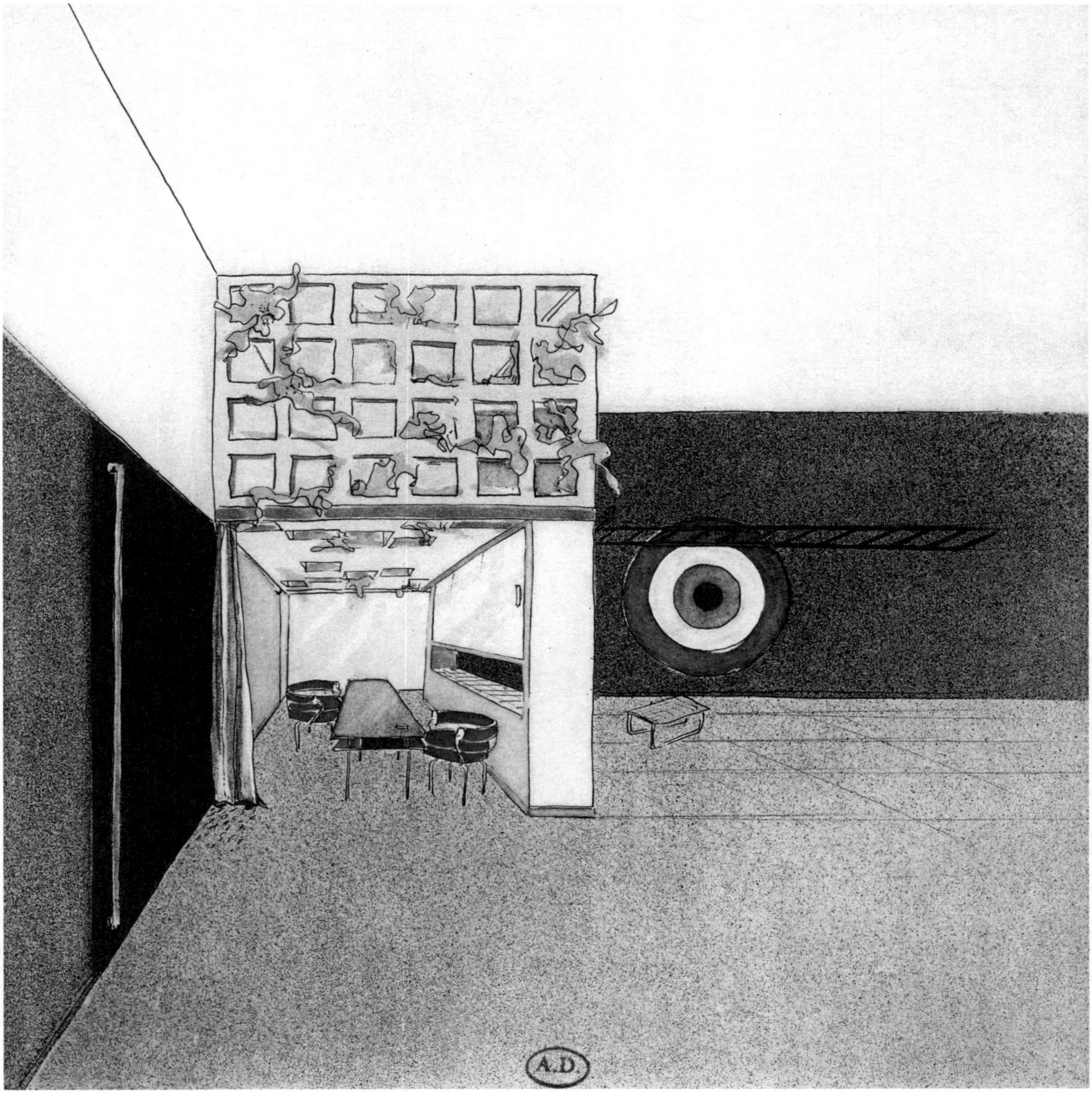

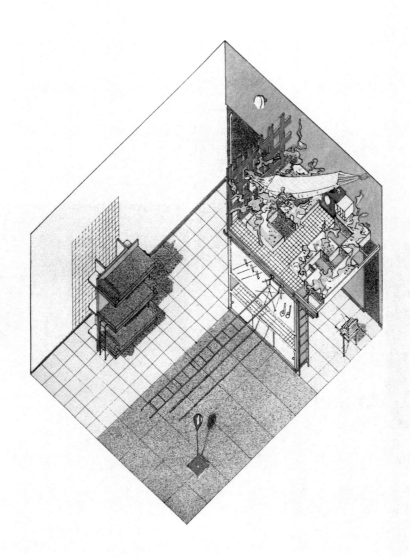

Fig. 40

Fig. 41

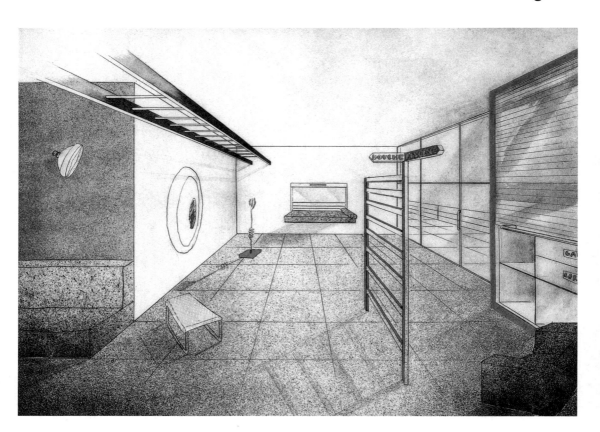

Fig. 42

Fig. 43

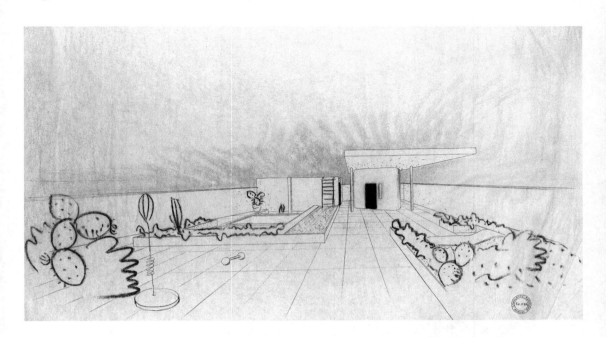

Fig. 43   In 1930, Perriand led the design of a private house in Buenos Aires for Le Corbusier's atelier. Her enthusiasm for physical culture was once again on full display, this time through the provision of a well-outfitted roof terrace with swimming pool and gymnastic equipment.

Fig. 44–45 Perriand, along with colleagues René Herbst and Louis Sognot, led the atelier's design and realization of a one-to-one mock-up for La Maison du Jeune Homme (House of a Young Man) for 1958's Exposition Universelle (Expo '58) in Brussels.

Fig. 45

Fig. 46 The thrilling ambiguity hinted at in Travail et Sport is legible once more in Perriand's photo of her own studio in Paris nearly a decade later, wherein a set of gymnastic rings hangs within reach of a small dining table.

Fig. 47 No space more clearly illustrates the martial fascination in physical culture during Mussolini's rule than the marble-lined Palestra del Duce by Luigi Moretti, in which statues of an idealized Roman man preside over a formally austere but materially sumptuous gymnasium.

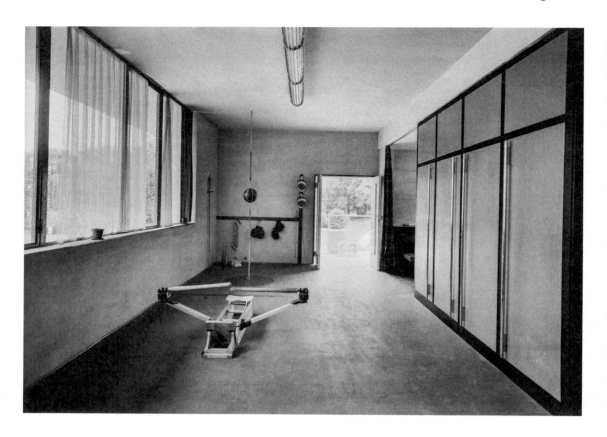

Fig. 48–50   One of a number of model houses built for the Triennale di Milano in 1933, the Casa dell'Aviatore—designed by Cesare Scoccimarro, Ermes Midena, and Piero Zanini—envisioned physical exercise as a crucial aspect of domestic life for the theoretical inhabitant, a military officer. The bedroom furniture includes a rowing machine and boxing equipment, and the airplane hangar on the ground floor could be accessed more rapidly via a sliding pole in the cylinder of the helix staircase.

Fig. 49–50

Fig. 51–52 The inclusion of a small gymnasium on one of the rooftop terraces in the house of Luigi Figini, one of Italy's leading rationalist architects, attests to the importance of physical culture in the modern formulation of daily life during this period. Here, Gege Figini, the architect's wife, poses with a set of gymnastic rings alongside a climbing rope. After a workout, members of the family could cool off on another of the terraces, where Figini installed a shallow pool and hammock alongside a diminutive patch of grass.

Fig. 52

Fig. 53–56 Franco Albini's Room for a Man, designed for the 1936 Triennale di Milano, condensed several activities he considered essential to modern living into the most compact space possible. Physical culture figured prominently in his considerations, and the space includes a rowing machine, a padded mat alongside a glass wall etched with instructional diagrams for calisthenics and stretches, and a locker with equipment for outdoor activities like hiking and climbing.

Fig. 54

Fig. 55

Fig. 56

Fig. 57–59 Influenced by his clients' dedication to new ideas about health and wellness, Richard Neutra integrated the Lovell Health House into the cliffside site in such a way that it would receive maximum exposure to the sun, and provided a series of programmed terraces for gymnastics, swimming, and sunbathing.

Fig. 58

Fig. 59

Fig. 60–63 Originally published at the architect's insistence as the Mensendieck House, this small house in Palm Springs was designed by Neutra for an American devotee of the German physician's system of applied gymnastics. One of the earliest of Neutra's "desert houses," the project seamlessly blends the client's living space with a dance studio, with only the use of mirrored surfaces to differentiate them.

Fig. 63

Fig. 64 Breuer's earlier fascination with integrating physical culture into the home was briefly resuscitated in his 1953 design for a "bathroom of the future" for use by the U.S. State Department.

Fig. 65–68   For the 1986 Triennale di Milano, Rem Koolhaas seized upon the modernist fascination with sport as a point of departure for his evocative Casa Palestra, in which he contorted the floor plan of Mies van der Rohe's Barcelona Pavilion to conform to OMA's peculiar, curved exhibition space.

Fig. 67–68

1792
Fig. 8
Gymnastik für die Jugend
Johann Christoph Friedrich
    GutsMuths
Germany
p. 57

1811
Fig.12
Turnplatz
Friedrich Jahn
Berlin, Germany
p. 61

1813
Fig. 9–11
Gymnastiska Centralinstitutet
Per Henrik Ling
Stockholm, Sweden
p. 58–60

1923–27
Fig. 34–37
Villa Noailles
Robert Mallet-Stevens
Hyères, France
p. 81–83, 114–115

1924
Gymnasium Addition for a
    Private School
Mies van der Rohe
Potsdam, Germany
p. 116–117

1925
Fig. 32–33
Villa Guggenbühl
    (Hôtel Particulier)
André Lurçat
Paris, France
p. 79–80, 118–119

1926
Fig. 14
Gret Palucca
p. 63

1926
Fig. 20–21
Piscator Apartment
Marcel Breuer
Berlin, Germany
p. 68–69

1927
Fig. 29
House 22, Weissenhof Estate
Richard Döcker
Stuttgart, Germany
p. 77, 120–121

1927
Fig. 16
The Jump Over the Bauhaus
Dessau, Germany
Photo by T. Lux Feininger
p. 65

1927 (published 1929)
Fig. 38–41
Travail et Sport
Charlotte Perriand
Unbuilt
p. 84–87, 122–123

1927 (published 1929)
Fig. 42
Salle de Culture Physique
Charlotte Perriand
Unbuilt
p. 88

1927–29
Fig. 57–59
Lovell Health House
Richard Neutra
Los Angeles, USA
p. 102–104

1928–30
Fig. 1–7
Villa Tugendhat
Mies van der Rohe
Brno, Czech Republic
Photos by Miloš Budík c.1956
p. 51–56, 124–125

1928–30
Fig. 15
Gymnasium, ADGB Trade
    Union School
Hannes Meyer and
    Hans Wittwer
Bernau-bei-Berlin, Germany
p. 64, 126–127

1929
Fig. 17–19
Karla Grosch / Physical
    Culture at the Bauhaus
Dessau, Germany
Photos by T. Lux Feininger
p. 66–67

1929
Fig. 30–31
House 26/27, WuWA Estate
Theo Effenberger
Wrocław, Poland (formerly
    Breslau, Germany)
p. 78, 128–129

1930
Fig. 22
Apartment for a Gymnastics
    Instructor
Marcel Breuer
Berlin, Germany
p. 70, 130

1930
Fig. 26–27
Werkbund Exhibition, Salon
    des Artistes Décorateurs
Walter Gropius, Marcel Breuer,
    and Herbert Bayer
Paris, France
p. 74–75

1930
Fig. 43
Villa Martínez de Hoz
Charlotte Perriand,
    Le Corbusier, and Pierre
    Jeanneret
p. 89

Figures Index

1931
Fig. 23–25
House for a Sportsman, Bauausstellung
Marcel Breuer
Berlin, Germany
p. 71–73, 131

1931
Fig. 28
Common Rooms for a High-rise Apartment Building, Bauausstellung
Walter Gropius
Berlin, Germany
p. 76, 132–133

1933
Fig. 48–50
Casa dell'Aviatore (House for an Aviator), Triennale di Milano
Cesare Scoccimarro, Ermes Midena, and Piero Zanini
Milan, Italy
p. 94–95, 134–135

1934
Fig. 51–52
Casa Figini
Luigi Figini
Milan, Italy
p. 96–97, 136–137

1935
Fig. 44–45
La Maison du Jeune Homme, Exposition Universelle
Charlotte Perriand, Le Corbusier, and Pierre Jeanneret
Brussels, Belgium
p. 90–91, 138

1936–37
Fig. 47
Palestra del Duce, Foro Italico
Luigi Moretti
Rome, Italy
p. 93

1936
Fig. 53–56
Room for a Man, Triennale di Milano
Franco Albini
Milan, Italy
p. 98–101, 139

1936–37
Fig. 60–63
Mensendieck House (Grace Lee Miller House)
Richard Neutra
Palm Springs, USA
p. 105–108, 140

1938
Fig. 46
Studio in Montparnasse
Charlotte Perriand
Paris, France
p. 92

1950s
Fig. 13
Mensendieck School
Oslo, Norway
p. 62

1953
Fig. 64
Prototype of Model Bathroom
Marcel Breuer
New York, USA
p. 109

1986
Fig. 65–68
Casa Palestra, Triennale di Milano
OMA / Rem Koolhaas
Milan, Italy
p. 110–111, 141

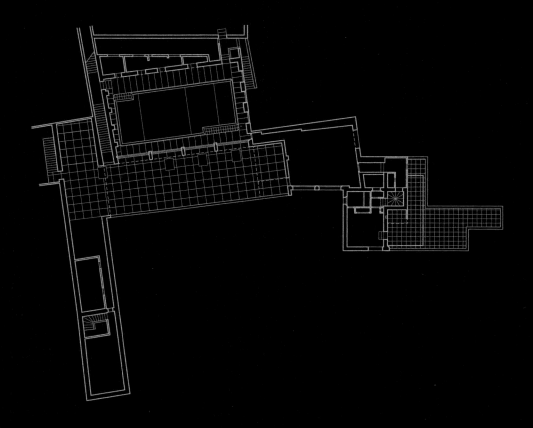

1923–27
Villa Noailles, Floor +2, Floor +2 (detail)
Robert Mallet-Stevens
Hyères, France
1:400, 1:200

Fig. 34–37 Reconstructed Plans

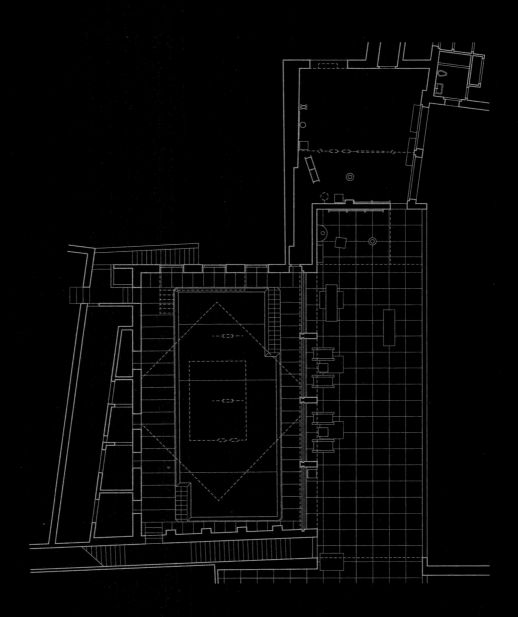

1924
Gymnasium Addition for a Private School
Mies van der Rohe
Potsdam, Germany
1:200

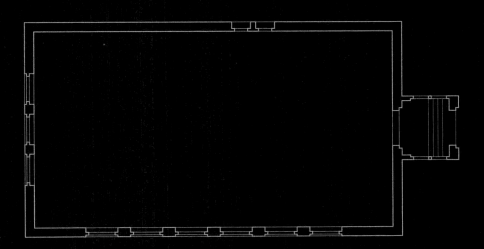

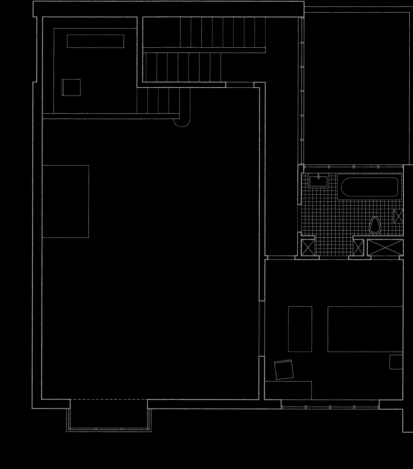

1925
Villa Guggenbühl (Hôtel Particulier), Floor +1, Floor +
André Lurçat
Paris, France
1:100

Fig. 32–33

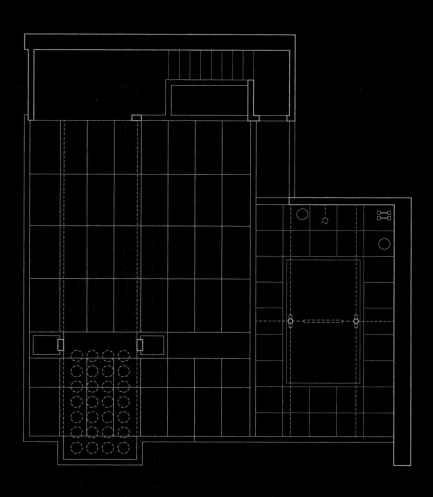

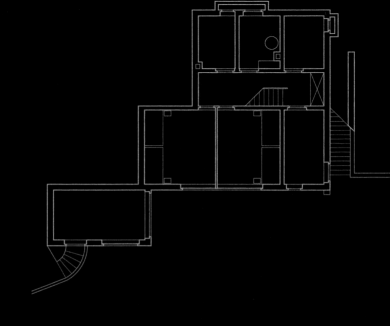

1927
House 22, Weissenhof Estate, Floor 0, Floor +1
Richard Döcker
Stuttgart, Germany
1:200

Fig. 29

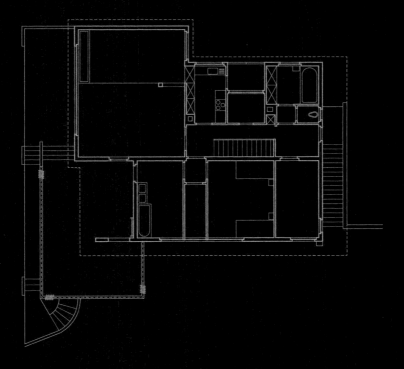

1927 (published 1929)
Travail et Sport
Charlotte Perriand
Unbuilt
1:100

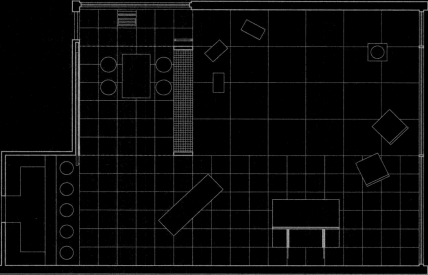

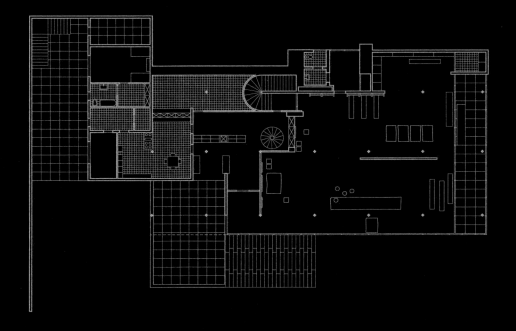

1928–30 (plan c. 1956)
Villa Tugendhat, Floor -1, Floor 0
Mies van der Rohe
Brno, Czech Republic
1:400

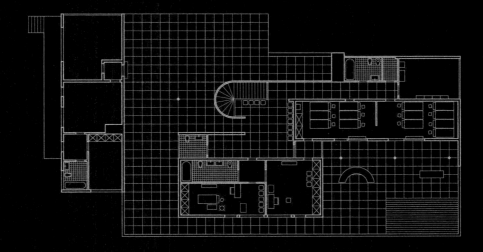

Fig. 1–7

1928–30
Gymnasium, ADGB Trade Union School
Hannes Meyer and Hans Wittwer
Bernau-bei-Berlin, Germany
1:200

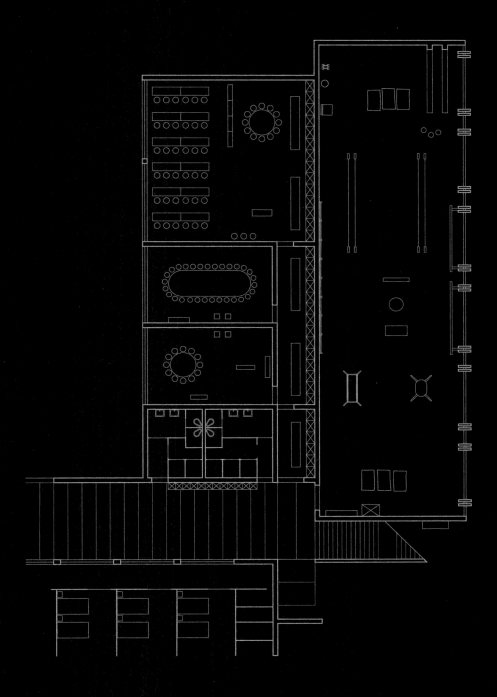
Fig. 15

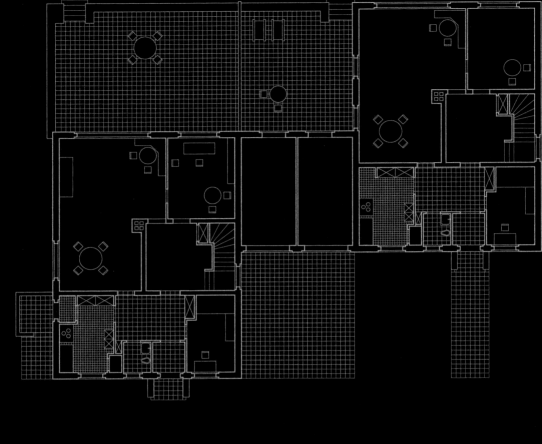

1929
House 26/27, WuWA Estate, Floor 0, Floor +1
Theo Effenberger
Wrocław, Poland (formerly Breslau, Germany)
1:200

Fig. 30–31

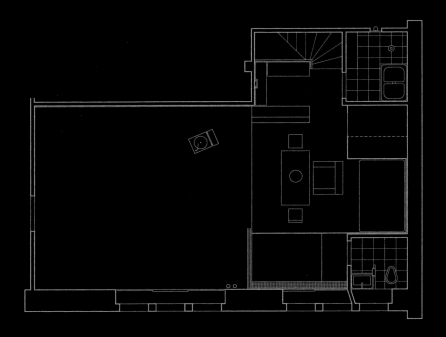

1930
Apartment for a Gymnastics Instructor
Marcel Breuer
Berlin, Germany
1:100

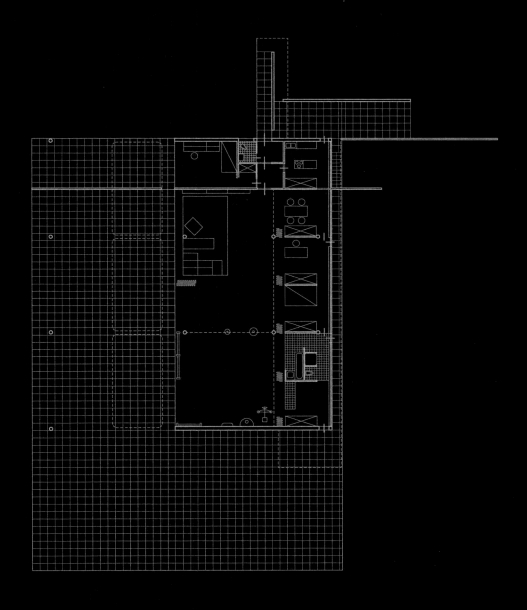

1931
House for a Sportsman, Bauausstellung
Marcel Breuer
Berlin, Germany
1:250

132

1931
Common Rooms, Bauausstellung
Walter Gropius
Berlin, Germany
1:250

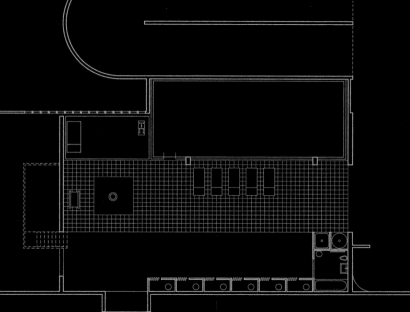

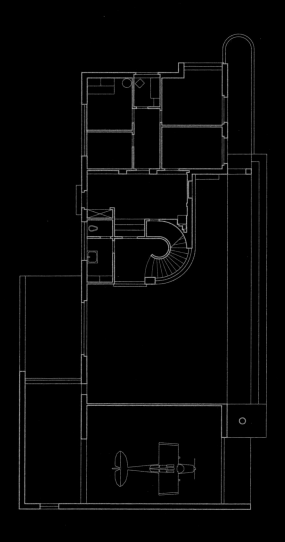

1933
Casa dell'Aviatore, Triennale di Milano, Floor 0, Floor +1
Cesare Scoccimarro, Ermes Midena, and Piero Zanini
Milan, Italy
1:200

Fig. 48–50

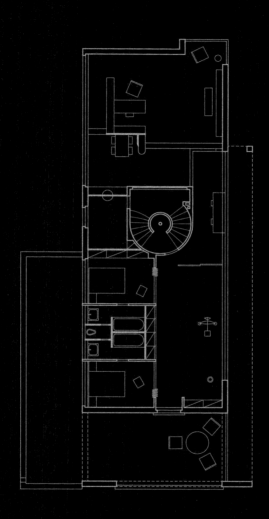

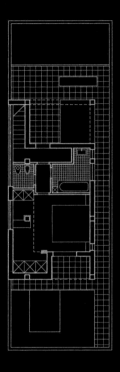

1934
Casa Figini, Floor +1, Floor +2
Luigi Figini
Milan, Italy
1:200

Fig. 51–52

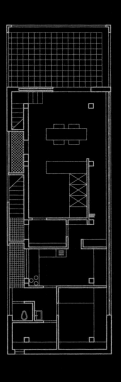

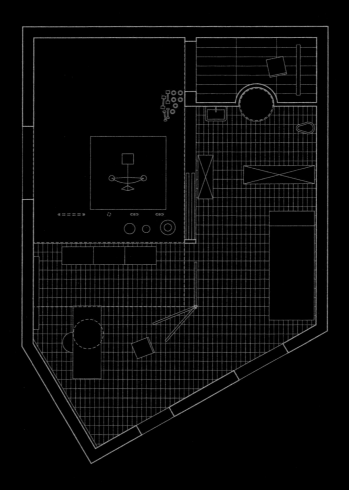

1935
La Maison du Jeune Homme, Exposition Universelle
Charlotte Perriand, Le Corbusier, Pierre Jeanneret
Brussels, Belgium
1:100

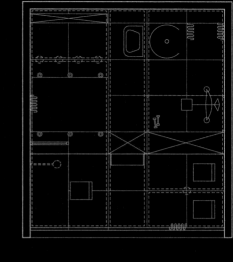

1936
Room for a Man, Triennale di Milano
Franco Albini
Milan, Italy
1:100

1936–37
Mensendieck House (Grace Lee Miller House)
Richard Neutra
Palm Springs, USA
1:200

Fig. 65–68   141

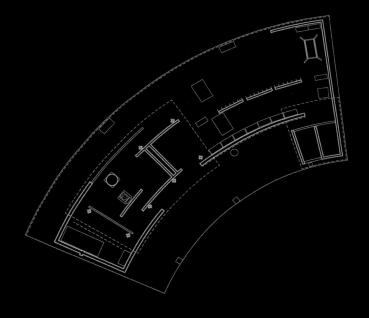

1986
Casa Palestra, Triennale di Milano
OMA / Rem Koolhaas
Milan, Italy
1:200

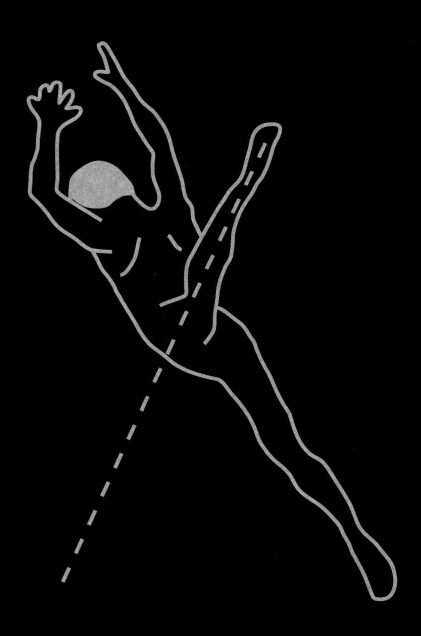

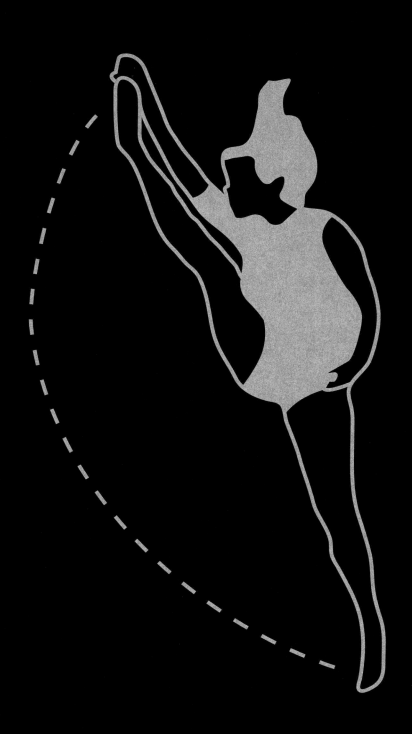

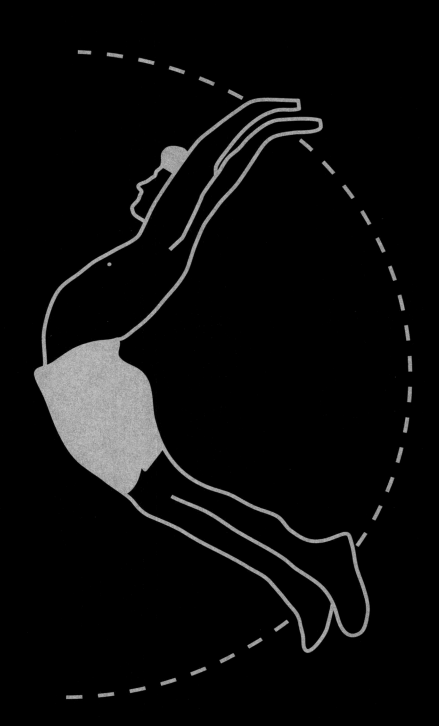

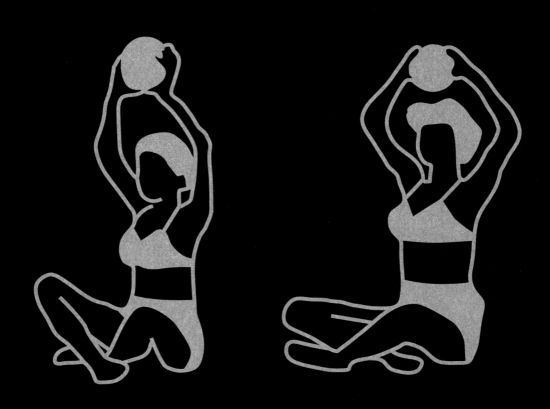

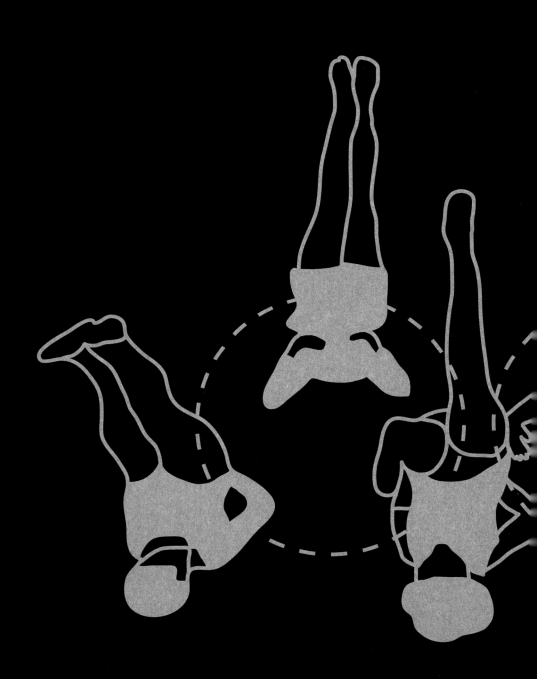

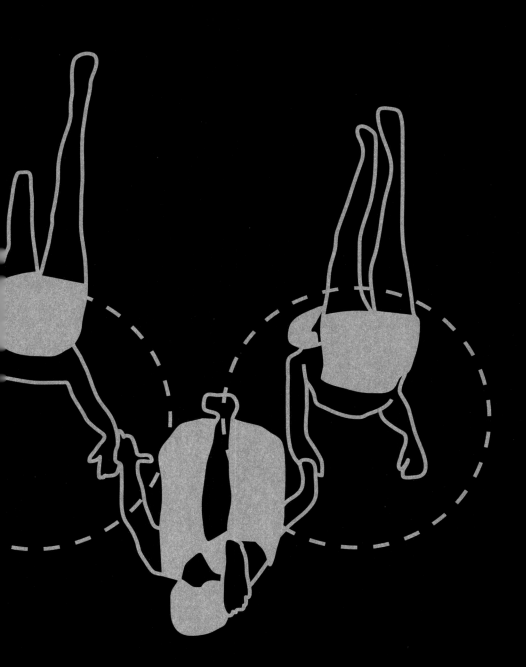

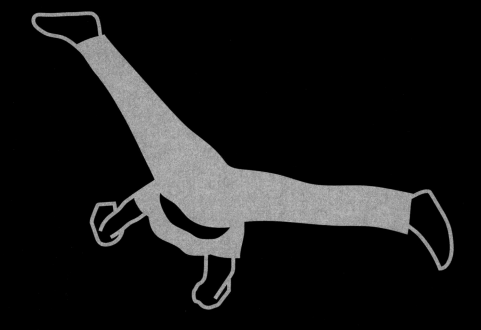

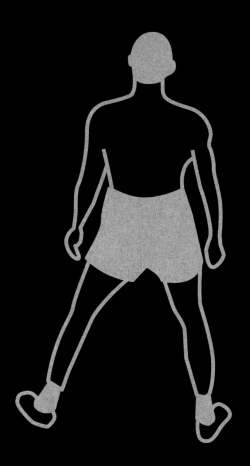

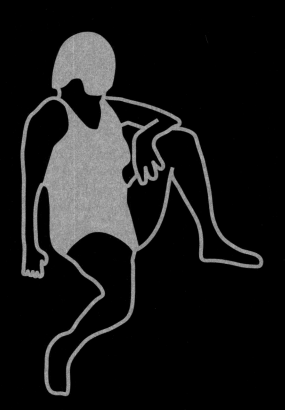

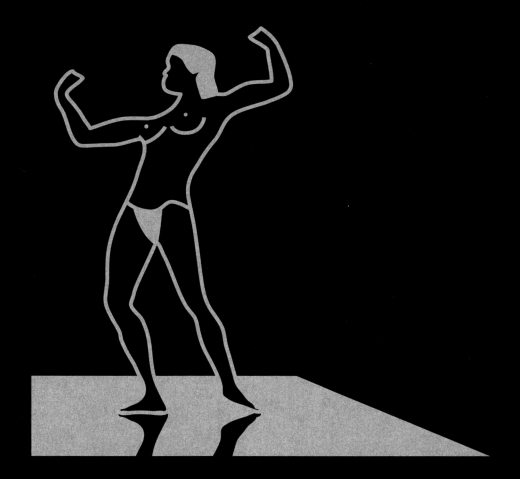

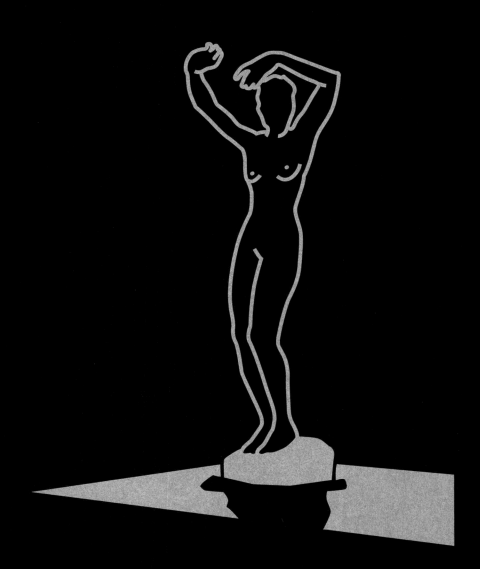

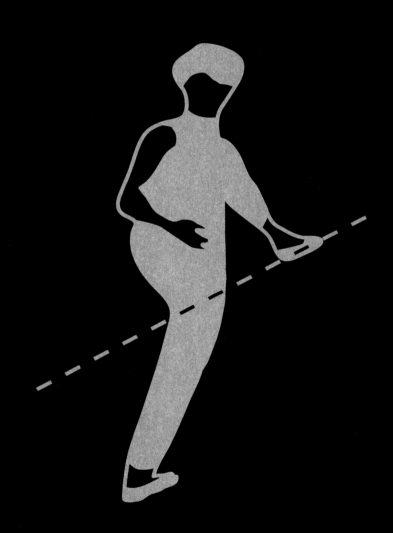

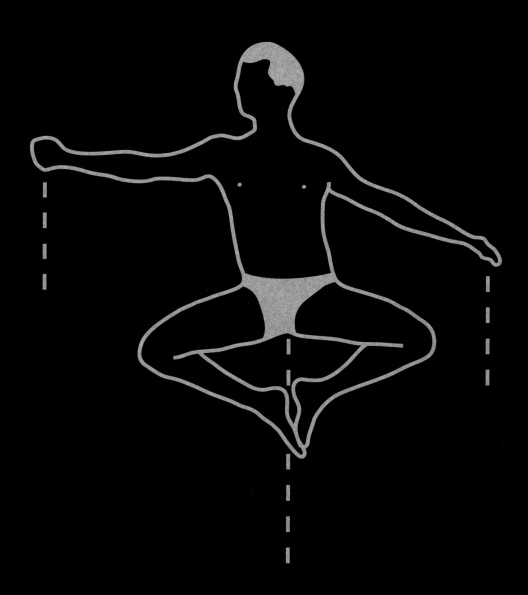

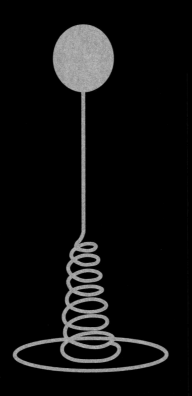
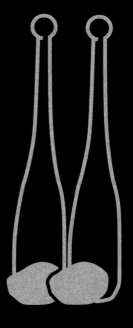

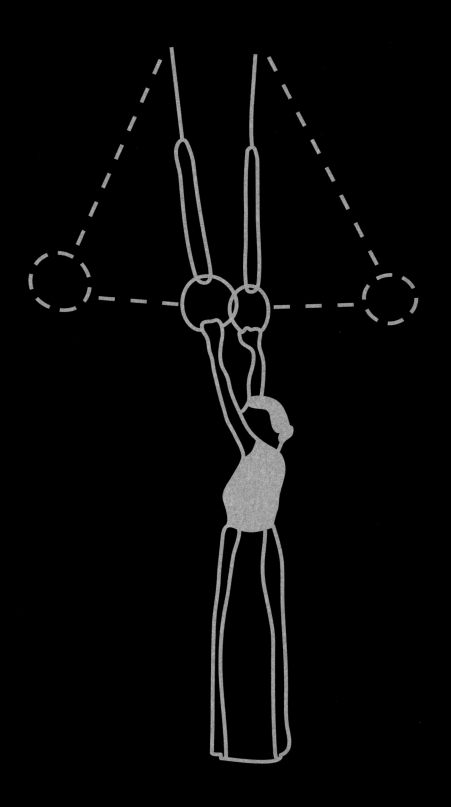

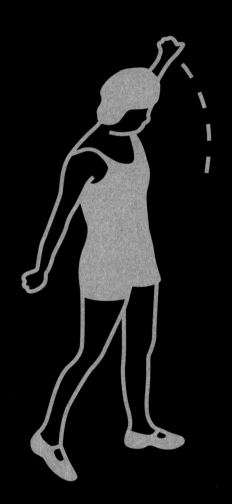

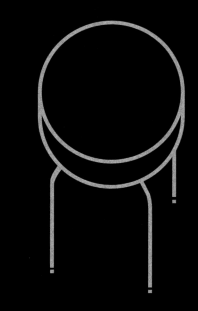

165

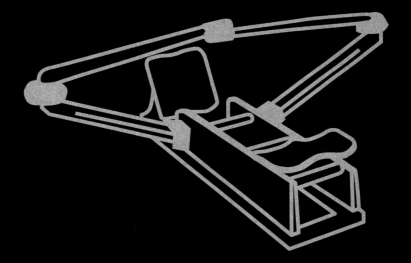

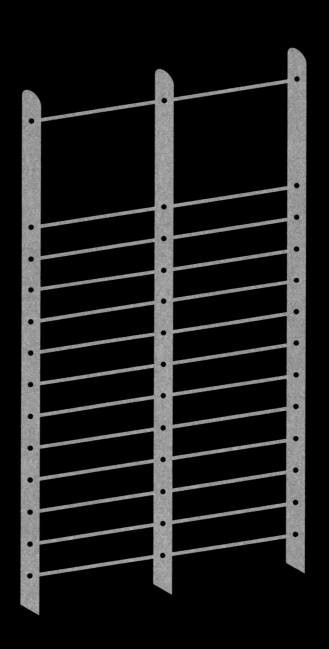

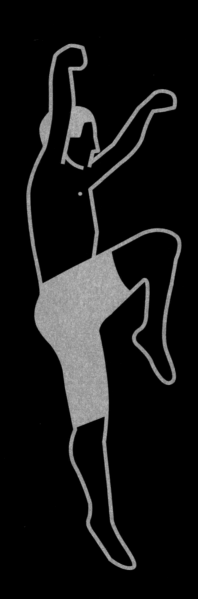

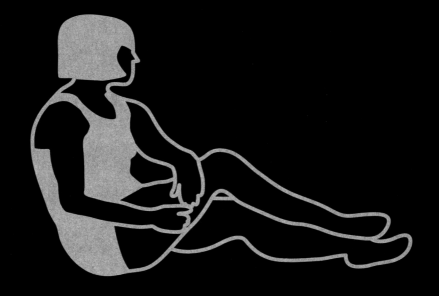

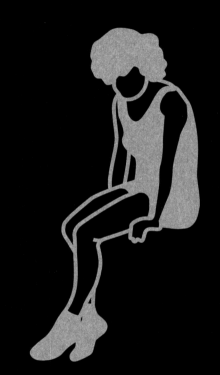

Ábalos, Iñaki. *The Good Life: A Guided Visit to the Houses of Modernity*. Zurich: Park Books, 2017.

Baker, William Joseph. *Sports in the Western World*. Urbana: University of Illinois Press, 1988.

Barsac, Jacques. *Charlotte Perriand: Complete Works*. Zurich: Scheidegger & Spiess, 2014.

Beachy, Robert. *Gay Berlin: Birthplace of a Modern Identity*. New York: Knopf Doubleday, 2014.

Blaser, Werner. *Mies van der Rohe*. Basel: Birkhäuser, 1997.

Briolle, Cécile, Agnès Fuzibet and Gérard Monnier. *La Villa Noailles: Rob Mallet-Stevens*. Marseille: Editions Parenthèses, 1990.

Bucci, Federico. *Franco Albini*. Milan: Electa, 2009.

Černá, Iveta and Dagmar Černoušková, eds. *Mies in Brno. Tugendhat House*. 2nd ed. Brno: Brno City Museum, 2018.

Černoušková, Dagmar and Jindřich Chatrný, eds. *Miloš Budík. Villa Tugendhat. 1956*. Brno: Brno City Museum, 2015.

Cohen, Jean-Louis. *André Lurçat, 1894–1970: l'autocritique d'un moderne*. Liège: Mardaga, 1995.

Cohen, Jean-Louis. *Mies Van Der Rohe*. London: E. & F.N. Spon, 1996.

Colomina, Beatriz. *Domesticity at War*. Cambridge, MA: MIT Press, 2007.

Cowan, Michael J. *Cult of the Will: Nervousness and German Modernity*. University Park: Penn State Press, 2008.

Dachs, Sandra, Patricia de Muga, and Laura Hintze, eds. *Charlotte Perriand: Objects and Furniture Design*. Barcelona: Ediciones Polígrafa, 2005.

Döcker, Richard. *Terrassen Typ : Krankenhaus, Erholungsheim, Hotel, Burohaus, Einfamilienhaus, Siedlungshaus, Meithaus und die Stadt*. Stuttgart: Julius Hoffmann Verlag, 1930.

Driller, Joachim. *Breuer Houses*. London: Phaidon, 2000.

Etlin, Richard A. *Modernism in Italian Architecture, 1890–1940*. Cambridge, MA: MIT Press, 1991.

Fiedler, Jeannine and Peter Feierabend. *Bauhaus*. Cologne: Könemann, 2000.

Fischer, Iris Smith. "The Role of Séméiotique in François Delsarte's Aesthetics." *Semiotica: Journal of the International Association for Semiotic Studies* 2018, no. 221 (February 2018): 12342. doi.org/10.1515/sem-2015-0153.

Frampton, Kenneth. *Modern Architecture: A Critical History*. London: Thames & Hudson, 2010.

Fricke, Roswitha, ed. *Bauhaus Fotografie*. Düsseldorf: Ed. Marzona, 1982.

Gay, Peter. *Weimar Culture: The Outsider as Insider*. New York: W.W. Norton, 2001.

Giedion, Sigfried. *Befreites Wohnen = Liberated Dwelling*. Edited by Reto Geiser and Rachel Julia Engler. Zurich: Lars Müller, 2019.

Grau, Andrée and Stephanie Jordan, eds. *Europe Dancing: Perspectives on Theatre, Dance, and Cultural Identity*. Abingdon: Routledge, 2010.

Gregotti, Vittorio, and Giovanni Marzari, eds. *Luigi Figini Gino Pollini: Opera Completa*. 2nd ed. Milan: Electa, 2002.

Hargreaves, Jennifer and Patricia Vertinsky, eds. *Physical Culture, Power, and the Body*. New York: Routledge, 2007.

Joly, Pierre. *L'architecte André Lurçat*. Paris: Picard, 1995.

Kaes, Anton Martin Jay and Edward Dimendberg. *The Weimar Republic Sourcebook*. Berkley: University of California Press, 1995.

Kant, Immanuel and E.F. Buchner. *The Educational Theory of Immanuel Kant*.

Philadelphia/London: J.B. Lippincott Co., 1908.

Kilston, Lyra. *Sun Seekers: The Cure of California*. Edited by Ananda Pellerin. Los Angeles, CA: Atelier Editions, 2019.

Koolhaas, Rem and Bruce Mau. *S,M,L,XL*. New York: Monacelli Press, 1995.

Kyle, Donald G. and Gary D. Stark, eds. *Essays on Sport History and Sport Mythology*. College Station: Texas A&M Press, 1990.

Lamprecht, Barbara Mac. *Richard Neutra: Complete Works*. New York: Taschen, 2000.

Lane, Barbara Miller. *Architecture and Politics in Germany: 1918–1945*. Cambridge, MA: Harvard University Press, 1968.

Lasansky, D. Medina. *Renaissance Perfected: Architecture, Spectacle, and Tourism in Fascist Italy (Buildings, Landscapes, and Societies)*. University Park, PA: Penn State University Press, 2005.

Leet, Steven. *Richard Neutra's Miller House*. New York: Princeton Architectural Press, 2004.

Lempa, Heikki. *Beyond the Gymnasium: Educating the Middle-class Bodies in Classical Germany*. Plymouth: Lexington Books, 2007.

Mangan, J.A., ed. *Sport in Europe: politics, class, gender*. London: Frank Cass, 1999.

Marhoefer, Laurie. *Sex and the Weimar Republic: German Homosexual Emancipation and the Rise of the Nazis*. Toronto: University of Toronto Press, 2015.

Markgraf, Monika, ed. *Archaeology of Modernism: Renovation Bauhaus Dessau = Archäologie Der Moderne: Sanierung Bauhaus Dessau*. Berlin: Jovis / Edition Bauhaus, 2006.

McCarter, Robert. *Breuer*. London: Phaidon, 2016.

McCoy, Esther. *Richard Neutra*. New York: G. Braziller, 1960.

Meyer, Hannes and Claude Schnaidt. *Hannes Meyer: Bauten, Projekte Und Schriften/Hannes Meyer: Buildings, Projects, and Writings*. Translated by D.Q. Stephenson. London: A. Tiranti, 1965.

Meyer, Hannes. "Die Neue Welt." *Das Werk : Architektur und Kunst* 13, no. 7 (July 1926): 205–24.

Meyer, Hannes. *Hannes Meyer 1889–1954: Architekt, Urbanist, Lehrer*. Berlin: Ernst & Sohn, 1989.

Mosse, George L. *The Image of Man: The Creation of Modern Masculinity*. New York: Oxford University Press, 2010.

Müller, Lars, ed. *Bauhaus Journal 1926–1931: Facsimile Edition*. Zurich: Lars Müller, Berlin: Bauhaus-Archiv / Museum für Gestaltung, 2019.

Norberg-Schulz, Christian. *Casa Tugendhat/Tugendhat House: Brno*. Rome: Officina Edizioni, 1984.

Naul, Roland. *Olympic Education*. Maidenhead: Meyer and Meyer, 2008.

May, Otto. *Friedrich Ludwig Jahn und die Turnbewegung*. Hildesheim: Franzbecker, 2015.

Perriand, Charlotte. *Charlotte Perriand: Interior Equipment*. New York: Architectural League of New York, 1997.

Pica, Agnoldomenico. *Storia della Triennale, 1918–1957*. Milan: Edizioni del Milione, 1957.

Piva, Antonio. *Franco Albini, 1905–1977*. Milan: Electa, 1998.

Plossu, Bernard and François Carrassan. *L'improbable destin de la Villa Noailles*. Marseille: Images en manoeuvres, 2010.

Poppelreuter, Tanja. "Social Individualism: Walter Gropius and His Appropriation of Franz Muller-Lyers Idea of a New Man." *Journal of Design History*, 24, no. 1 (2011): 37–58. doi.org/10.1093/jdh/epq049

Porte, Alain. *François Delsarte: une anthologie*. Paris: Ipmc, 1992.

Protasoni, Sara. *Figini e Pollini: Architetture 1927–1989*. Milano: Electa, 2010.

Quick, Robert Herbert. *Essays on Educational Reformers*. New York: E.L. Kellogg and Co, 1890.

Rado, Lisa, ed. *Modernism, Gender, and Culture: A Cultural Studies Approach*. New York: Routledge, 1997.

Riley, Terence, and Barry Bergdoll. *Mies in Berlin*. New York, NY: Museum of Modern Art, 2001.

Rossi Prodi, Fabrizio. *Franco Albini*. Rome: Officina, 1996.

Rousseau, Jean-Jacques. *Emile: or On Education* (1763). Translated by Allan Bloom. New York: Basic Books, 1979.

Rüegg, Arthur. *Charlotte Perriand: Livre De Bord, 1928–1933*. Basel: Birkhäuser, 2004.

Salmon, Jacqueline. *Robert Mallet-Stevens et la villa Noailles à Hyères*. Paris: Marval, 2005.

Scharenberg, Swantje. "Physical Education at the Bauhaus, 1919–33." *The International Journal of the History of Sport* 20, no. 3 (2003): 115–27. doi:10.1080/09523360412331305813.

Schuldenfrei, Robin. *Luxury and Modernism: Architecture and the Object in Germany 1900–1933*. Princeton: Princeton University Press, 2018.

Schumacher, Thomas L. *Surface and Symbol: Giuseppe Terragni and the Architecture of Italian Rationalism*. New York: Princeton Architectural Press, 1991.

Sendai, Shoichiro. "The Conception of 'Equipment' by Charlotte Perriand: Crossover between Le Corbusier and Japan." *Journal of Asian Architecture and Building Engineering*, 18, no. 5 (2019): 430–38.

Shawn, Ted. *Every Little Movement: A Book about François Delsarte, the Man and his Philosophy, his Science and Applied Aesthetics, the Application of this Science to the Art of the Dance, the Influence of Delsarte on American Dance*. Pennington, NJ: Dance Horizons/Princeton Book Co, 1988.

Stebbins, Genevieve. *Delsarte System of Expression*. 2nd ed. New York: Edgar S. Werner, 1887.

Teyssot, Georges. *A Topology of Everyday Constellations*. Cambridge, MA: MIT Press, 2013.

Toepfer, Karl. *Empire of Ecstasy: Nudity and Movement in German Body Culture, 1910–1935*. Berkeley: University of California Press, 1997.

Urbanik, Jadwiga. *WuWA, 1929–2009: The Werkbund Exhibition in Wrocław*. Wrocław: Muzeum Architektury we Wrocławiu, 2010.

Volpi, Cristiana. *Robert Mallet-Stevens: 1886–1945*. Milan: Electa, 2005.

Wingler, Hans Maria. *Bauhaus: Weimar, Dessau, Berlin, Chicago*. Cambridge, MA: MIT Press, 1969.

Thanks

Michael Abel
Amale Andraos
Verena Andric
Pep Avilés
Jacques Barsac
Juan Benavides
Barbora Benčíková
Matthew Brubaker
Miloš Budík
Adam Charlap-Hyman
Jean-Louis Cohen
Jesse Connuck
Laura Coombs
Conrad Feininger
Ryan Fierro
Kenneth Frampton
Melissa Frost
Letizia Garzoli
Reto Geiser
Ayesha Ghosh
Sharon Gong
James Graham
Grete Grubelich
Andre Herrero
Isabelle Hyman
Sharon Johnston
Isabelle Kirkham-Lewitt
Silvia Kolbowski
Thomas Kramer
Mark Lee
Sharon Leung
Sibylle Le Vot
Daniele Mainetti

Werner Möller
Noemi Mollet
Pernette Perriand Barsac
Sofia Rodríguez Abbud
Hilary Sample
Patrick Schneebeli
Lisa Schons
Domenica Schulz
Peter Sima-Eichler
Leopoldo Villardi
Lucy Weisner
Lindsey Wikstrom
Sondra Wittwer
Alicja Wodzińska
Lulu Wolf
Su Wu

Lastly, thanks to our families.

Image Credits

Fig. 1–7
© 2023 Miloš Budík.

Fig. 8
Creative Commons CC BY 4.0. Courtesy of the Wellcome Collection.

Fig. 9–11
Public Domain. Courtesy of the Library of the GIH—The Swedish School of Sport and Health Sciences, Stockholm.

Fig. 12
Public Domain. Courtesy of Ullstein Bild.

Fig. 13
Public Domain. Courtesy of the National Library of Norway.

Fig. 14
Public Domain. Photograph by Franz Fiedler.

Fig. 15
Courtesy of gta Archiv / ETH Zürich, Haefeli Moser Steiger.

Fig. 16–19
© Estate of T. Lux Feininger. Courtesy of Bauhaus-Archiv Berlin.

Fig. 20–25
Courtesy of Marcel Breuer Papers, Special Collections Research Center, Syracuse University Libraries.

Fig. 26–28
© 2023 Artists Rights Society (ARS), New York / ProLitteris, Zurich. Courtesy of Bauhaus-Archiv Berlin.

Fig. 29
Courtesy of Avery Classics, Avery Architectural & Fine Arts Library, Columbia University.

Fig. 30–31
Courtesy of the Museum of Architecture in Wrocław.

Fig. 32–33
© 2023 Artists Rights Society (ARS), New York / ADAGP, Paris. Courtesy of Fonds Lurçat. CNAM/SIAF / Cité de l'architecture et du patrimoine / Archives d'architecture du XXe siècle.

Fig. 34–37
Courtesy of Avery Classics, Avery Architectural & Fine Arts Library, Columbia University.

Fig. 38–46
© 2023 Artists Rights Society (ARS), New York / ADAGP, Paris. Courtesy of Archives Charlotte Perriand.

Fig. 47
Courtesy of L'Archivio Centrale dello Stato (ACS), Archivio Moretti.

Fig. 48–50
© 2023 Triennale Milano—Archivio Fotografico.

Fig. 51–52
Courtesy of MART, Archivio del '900, Fondo Figini-Pollini. Photograph by Studio Crimella (Milan).

Fig. 53–56
© 2023 Triennale Milano—Archivio Fotografico.

Fig. 57
Courtesy of Avery Classics, Avery Architectural & Fine Arts Library, Columbia University.

Fig. 58–63
© J. Paul Getty Trust. Getty Research Institute, Los Angeles (2004.R.10).

Fig. 64
Courtesy of Marcel Breuer Papers, Special Collections Research Center, Syracuse University Libraries.

Fig. 65–68
© 2023 OMA.